Thriving through
MINISTRY CONFLICT

JAMES P. OSTERHAUS, JOSEPH M. JURKOWSKI, AND TODD A HAHN

Thriving through
MINISTRY CONFLICT

By Understanding Yur RED and BLUE Zones

ZONDERVAN™

GRAND RAPIDS, MICHIGAN 49530 USA

We want to hear from you. Please send your comments about this book to us in care of zreview@zondervan.com. Thank you.

ZONDERVAN™

Thriving through Ministry Conflict
Copyright © 2005 by TAG—The Armstrong Group

Published in association with Eames Literary Services, Nashville, Tennessee

Requests for information should be addressed to:
Zondervan, *Grand Rapids, Michigan 49530*

Library of Congress Cataloging-in-Publication Data

Osterhaus, James P.
    Thriving through ministry conflict : by understanding your red and blue zones / James P. Osterhaus, Joseph M. Jurkowski, and Todd A. Hahn.
       p. cm.
    Includes bibliographical references.
    ISBN-10: 0-310-26344-1 (hard : alk. paper)
    ISBN-13: 978-0-310-26344-9 (hardcover)
    1. Church controversies. 2. Clergy—Psychology. 3. Pastoral theology.
    I. Jurkowski, Joseph M. II. Hahn, Todd, 1968- III. Title.
    BV652.9.O88 2005
    253—dc22
                                                2005010114

This edition printed on acid-free paper.

The website addresses recommended throughout this book are offered as a resource to you. These websites are not intended in any way to be or imply an endorsement on the part of Zondervan, nor do we vouch for their content for the life of this book.

Interior design by Nancy Wilson

Printed in the United States of America

05 06 07 08 09 10 11 12 /❖ DCI/ 10 9 8 7 6 5 4 3 2 1

To our wives and children,
Anita, Marcy, David, Eddie, Justin, Jonathan,
whose loving spirits live in these pages

Contents

List of Response Activities

Acknowledgments

We would like to acknowledge the following people who read early versions of the manuscript and provided helpful suggestions and real encouragement: Jeff Cutruzzula, Dana Dixon, Mike Moses, Jenna Peeler, Dan Southerland, Dave Verhaagen, and Richard Wilson. Staci Marinack was involved with feedback chapter by chapter, and her constant encouragement and support were indispensable. Thanks to all of these friends and encouragers.

Introduction

A Dangerous and Difficult Path

The pathway of leadership is dangerous and difficult. This is doubly true for the man or woman in ministry. Take a look at this true story.

An Exhausted Pastor

Pastor Phil had good reason for his anxiety. His three-year ministry at a small midwestern church was shaping up to be a colossal failure. He had run up against a brick wall the likes of which few in ministry had experienced. A small but influential group in this aging, ingrown congregation of two hundred had early on tangled with Pastor Phil over the changes he was bringing to the church. Over time, he had become sensitive to their repeated criticisms and had finally worn to the breaking point.

In any organization, voices of dissent provide clues about unexpressed pain within the organization. However, these voices are often misinterpreted by the leaders of the organization because they are seen as oppositional. It is hard to hear the message when one feels personally attacked, when every action is questioned and every good idea is opposed.

Pastor Phil found himself in this very dilemma. He didn't understand the resistance to his initiatives, since most of the parishioners apparently agreed with his values and vision. No matter what he had tried, no matter how he had handled conflicts, the situation had grown steadily worse, and he and his family had suffered. This suffering had created doubt in Pastor Phil, doubt about his ability to lead and doubt about his vocation. As he had grown more and more depressed, he had also struggled with growing bitterness and resentment.

The search committee which had called him knew they needed a leader who would challenge the church community. They knew

Pastor Phil would confront contradictions in beliefs and behaviors; they knew he would never compromise his integrity. They wanted Pastor Phil to do what they could not do.

Pastor Phil's great error was innocence. He never understood that integrity is not necessarily valued, or that it is not a formula for popularity. He naively thought that new ideas would be greeted with enthusiasm. He thought that the long-term interests of the many would always win over the short-term interests of the few. He thought that because the community needed and said they wanted change, they would embrace it, and that in appreciation for his efforts, they would embrace him and his family. Instead, as he confronted the contradictions he saw in the church, he was attacked. He felt betrayed and wounded, and he personalized the attacks, which not only confused him but created shame and guilt in the members of the parish.

The church had been doing things in certain ways for years and had never been confronted about their behavior by previous pastors. They in turn felt wounded, betrayed, and personally attacked by Pastor Phil. They didn't understand what he was doing or why he was upset.

As time passed, Pastor Phil was worn down. He could not tone down the conflict, depersonalize the attacks coming at him, or rebuild relationships within the congregation. Finally, he left the church.

Faulty Expectations and Intense Personal Conflict

Between the three of us, we have over seventy years of experience working with pastors and churches, serving on church staffs, and fulfilling the role of pastor. We have found Pastor Phil's story to be the rule and not the exception. Good men and women with a calling for the Lord's work become exhausted, then defeated, and finally leave the ministry.

It is our observation that the average minister is

- highly committed,
- confused by the unrealistic expectations of others,
- and overwhelmed and frightened by incomprehensible conflict.

What goes wrong for pastors everywhere, over and over again? Faulty expectations that lead to intense personal conflict.

Adjust Expectations, Don't Satisfy Them

Here's an interesting paradox. The more pastors care, the more they are set up to fail. The reason they fail is because they tend to make perhaps the most serious error a leader can make. They attempt to meet all of the expectations of their congregation.

This attempt has two consequences:

1. Leaders run themselves ragged and destroy their own lives and the lives of their family members.
2. Leaders send the wrong message to their congregations, and especially to those needy individuals who have a great deal of woundedness from the past. This message is, "Yes, I can do it all. I can heal those wounds. I'm the right person for you." But sending this message is a recipe for disaster because leaders invariably are unable to meet all of their congregants' expectations.

So what's the answer to this dilemma? How can the pastor deal effectively with the congregation, and especially those deeply wounded people who want, who demand, that he or she heal all of their wounds, fix their defects, and compensate for their deficiencies?

It's not that ministers necessarily need to care less. What we recommend is caring within legitimate expectations. Quite simply, the task is not to meet unrealistic expectations. And we're not just talking about the unrealistic expectations of others. We're also talking about the unrealistic expectations we have of ourselves, expectations that we are often unaware that we have. The task is to adjust those unrealistic expectations first in ourselves and then in others.

But it is here, in the area of meeting expectations, that we find ministers have the most difficulty, and the least amount of competence, handling relational situations within their parishes. And so unmet expectations inevitably lead to personal conflict.

Conflict: Friend or Foe?

Most ministers run from conflict. And yet they are constantly drawn into it, despite taking every possible measure to avoid it. Books written to assist ministers often paint the congregation and the ruling board as the enemy of the minister. But we have a different view. Consider these points:

- Conflict is inescapable. Given differences in gender, background, cultural distinctiveness, and personality, it's no wonder we disagree a lot.
- The problem is not conflict, per se, but how people relate to one another when they're in conflict.
- Conflict is a good and necessary thing:
  - It elicits different points of view.
  - It clears the air.
  - It leads to the resolution of complex issues.

We know ministry is dangerous. Anyone who has been in it for more than a few months knows this. But we have also found that the hopeless patterns into which we fall can be understood and turned to redemptive purposes.

Thriving through Conflict

This book is about surviving and thriving in the places to which God has called you to minister. We're going to take a look at the two greatest challenges facing ministry leaders—faulty expectations and personal conflict—and what links them. And we're going to guide you through the three simple principles indispensable to any successful minister, whether ordained or lay. To accomplish these goals, we have chosen to tell a fictional story, a story similar to Pastor Phil's. Through this story, you will learn the principles everyone who is in ministry needs to know to survive and thrive through conflict.

After you have finished chapters 1–9, we encourage you to spend time working through the response activities in the back of the book, either by yourself or in a group, to help you implement these principles in your ministry.

Hold on now! Get ready. This book is going to begin and end with you.

CHAPTER 1

Welcome to the Jungle

B arry Wolf was getting used to the headaches. They started in the back of his head and worked their way relentlessly to a point behind his eyes so that no amount of kneading his temples helped. When a headache hit, he had to accept the misery until sleep or half a bottle of ibuprofen kicked in. It was no way to live if one wanted to lead a church effectively. And Barry was all about effectiveness.

After a ten-year career in insurance sales, Barry had come to the conclusion that God wanted him to become a pastor. Packing up his family, including two kids, Barry moved across the country for ministerial studies. Putting his rare combination of people skills and organizational acumen to work, Barry finished school early and landed his first pastorate, leading the First Community Church of Elizabethton, Illinois.

Barry had moved into his first call with the conviction that churches in the twenty-first century should be more than traditional chaplaincies and social clubs for the spiritually minded. He believed that the church should have an impact in the community and should function as an effective, life-changing organization by leading people to follow Christ closely and to live that out in their day-to-day lives. Barry wasn't sure how to make this happen, but he had both theological and commonsense business training and figured he could work it out in the field.

The call process had been a fairly straightforward one. Jim Grendell, the chairman of the search committee, combined the precision of a veteran CPA with the winsomeness of a gifted salesman. He was also refreshingly honest, even blunt, qualities that Barry admired, even if his own people-pleasing tendencies occasionally prevented him from practicing them.

"Look," said Jim, "I believe that you are the man for this job. You are in your midthirties, so you are not wet behind the ears. At the same time, this is your first pastorate, so you are not coming in with a lot of preconceptions. You also have a background as a salesperson, which you are going to need to turn this church around."

Jim described a church whose best days were behind it but which had potential for the future. First Community had been founded during the church boom years of the 1950s and had grown quickly. Located in a fairly affluent suburb of Chicago, the church attracted a wide spectrum of members, from young families to retirees. Its programs for children were known throughout the area, it boasted a series of gifted pastors, and the church made a significant contribution toward meeting the needs of the disadvantaged in the community.

The church's growth stabilized in the mid-1960s and stayed level for about another decade. In the 1970s the demographics of the community began to change as many families moved a bit farther away from the Chicago center. Those left behind tended to be older folks who had no desire to move and those who could not afford to move. In time the ethnic composition of the area began to change as well, and First Community, which had been mostly white, did not reflect this change. By the early 1990s the sanctuary, which seated 700 and had been filled nearly to capacity for years, held about 225 worshipers on Sunday morning, and the median age of the congregation was spiking upward.

Driven in part by the economic boom of the mid- to late-1990s, young families began to repopulate Elizabethton, but again the church wasn't able to attract this new population. By 2000, when Barry took the reins as pastor, the church's beautiful structure and rich history belied its decline in members, finances, and energy.

Barry was not one to shy away from a challenge and so had had no difficulty deciding to come to First Community. With Jim's stated support and the sense of the search committee that Barry was the one to lead the church in its efforts to reach young families and so revitalize itself, Barry and his family had moved to Elizabethton with high hopes and trust in God.

The next three years had been the longest of Barry's life. The congregation's worship seemed lifeless. There was a shortage of volunteers in every area. Offerings provided enough money to pay salaries and keep the building up, but there were few resources to expand ministry and create new programs, things Barry knew were essential to reach the changing community.

Worst of all, some of his early allies had become antagonists. The search committee had invited him specifically because he was young and creative and they knew the church needed to change. But when Barry began to implement changes—even minor ones to make the worship services livelier and to brighten the children's ministry rooms—he met resistance that seemed wholly out of proportion to his decisions.

The great shock was that Jim Grendell had become his nemesis.

Five minutes into Barry's first board meeting at First Community Church, it was clear who called the shots—Jim. Jim was not a physically imposing man, but he had a presence about him. He could talk to anyone about nearly everything and did so with charm. He was well spoken, was looked to as a mentor by many, and in spite of his apparent strength was given to emotion and even tears when discussing an issue important to him. And usually others followed him.

Jim was the kind of guy you wanted on your side and the exact person you hoped and prayed wasn't aligned against you, because, Barry soon realized, Jim took no prisoners when something stood between him and his goals. And within a year Jim's apparent goal was to ensure that anything Barry proposed was shot down in flames.

Barry and his wife, Sophia, sometimes sat up late at night as Barry tried to divine what could have caused the change in Jim, at least the change that Barry perceived. Was Jim threatened by Barry? Was he insecure? Was he manipulative? Had he lied when he recruited Barry by saying the church wanted change, and then did everything he could to block change? Had Barry missed something? And most often, what could Barry *do* to get around Jim's obstructionism or to change the way Jim led in the church?

Now, Barry was ready to pack it in. The board was stalemated. Attendance was static. Finances were mediocre. And Jim's campaign had taken on a new form—personal attacks against Barry. Barry heard the whispers. The pastor isn't what he appears to be. He takes a lot of long lunches, and doesn't it seem that pastors get a lot more time off than us working people? Why does he want to change everything around here? Who does he think he is? And according to some, Jim would occasionally tear up and say, "I had such hopes for him, for this church. But I think I was wrong. I am not at all sure that Barry is up to the task." All the while, in public, Jim presented himself as Barry's best friend and confidant.

All in all, Barry had led well and there were many in the church who supported him. The intrigue was mostly on the leadership level. But the conflict was killing Barry as board meetings turned into war zones, and initiatives which Barry felt were crucial died in subcommittees or mysteriously disappeared during the implementation phase.

In their late-night chats, Barry and Sophia had begun to talk about moving on. What most people didn't know was that behind his outgoing and friendly demeanor, Barry was a bit of a loner, prone to depression, and consumed with making others happy. He had never been able to understand these impulses fully, and now he knew he was paying the price for not paying attention. Sophia was wise, compassionate, a good listener, and strong. She encouraged him to hang in there, to do what he knew to be right, and to be patient. But Barry wasn't so sure he could anymore.

CHICAGO HAS A LOT OF FREEZING GRAY DAYS in January, and this was one of them. Barry was in his office at the church, staring out the window at the warehouse directly across the street. Jim Grendell owned the warehouse and sometimes worked out of its small office, and this had become a constant reminder to Barry of the man's seeming omnipresence in Barry's life. The warehouse was an ugly thing, stark and unattractive, and surrounded by a barbed-wire laced fence.

Barry spun his office chair away from the window and faced the half-written resignation letter on his laptop screen. He wasn't sure he would submit it this week at the board meeting, but he surely wanted to have it ready to print out, just in case.

On impulse he picked up his phone, hit the 9 key and punched in the number of his friend of nearly twenty years, Henry Grigg. Barry and Henry had been roommates in college, bonding almost immediately over their love for '80s hair-band music and the fact that both of them had emotionally absent fathers who had died before their sons had really got to know them. They laughed at their college musical tastes now, even as they realized as they got older how truly significant their incomplete relationships with their fathers were. Through the years, Henry and Barry had been a constant support for one another, and support was what Barry needed now.

"What's up, punk?" answered Henry, and Barry chuckled at how caller ID had changed how we all deal with our telephones. But as much as he loved Henry's sense of humor, Barry was in no mood and said immediately that he needed to talk seriously.

Henry was all ears as Barry told his story in detail, emphasizing his discouragement and the near-monster he perceived Jim Grendell to be. When Barry had finished, there was silence for a long moment, broken by Henry's low whistle.

"Man," Henry said, "you have drawn a tough hand. Do you want to quit?"

Barry was surprised by how quickly he answered "Yes!" and then caught himself. "I mean I feel like it, but I am also convinced that God wanted me here and that my work here is not done. I just can't see being anything but ineffective and depressed because of this guy Jim and those he influences. I'm letting my thirties get away from me dealing with this stuff and giving this guy rent-free space in my head even when I'm not sitting across a meeting table from him."

"You know how much I hate quick advice," said Henry. "But I'm going to offer some anyway," he said, laughing gently. "You have to call an old friend of mine, a guy named Elliott Stevens. He helped me out a lot early in my career and was great at getting me to ask the right questions without forcing answers down my throat. I mean, he can be really blunt, and that is painful sometimes, but I still consult him over major decisions. He is a seriously good encourager."

Barry hesitated. "I barely have the energy to pick up the phone and call you, much less—"

"Just drop a dime on him," Henry interrupted. "And drop my name. I know he will be willing to meet with you at least once. And what do you have to lose?"

And so Barry found himself outside a rather imposing brick house on a wooded lot in a peaceful, mostly underdeveloped suburb about forty-five minutes away. *He's got one of those heavy lion-head door knockers*, Barry thought. *Just great.*

As soon as Barry knocked, the door opened and Elliott Stevens was there. He smiled and invited Barry in, took his coat, pointed Barry toward his study, and went to get coffee.

ELLIOTT CAME INTO THE STUDY with two blue pottery cups and a stainless-steel thermos of steaming coffee. He wore crisply creased black pants, expensive Italian loafers, a light-blue Oxford shirt, and a black cardigan, which looked to be made of cashmere. His hair was presidentially white, and his eyes either blue or green—they seemed to change with the light, or what little there was as shadows fell in the comfortable book-lined study. He appeared to be anywhere from his early fifties to his late sixties in age.

Elliott sat in a leather wingback chair across from where Barry sank into a slightly overstuffed brown couch and fixed his eyes on his visitor. That was the first time Barry looked into his eyes, and even then he was struck by not only how their color changed but by how piercing they were, not quite threatening but not quite welcoming either.

"So, friend of Henry," Elliott began, "how can I be of service to you?"

Barry took a sip of his coffee and, a bit nervous, tried to make small talk.

"Oh, I don't know, really," he began. "I have heard Henry speak of you before and he thought we should get to know each other, thought you could be a good source of counsel for me. I guess I was wondering about your background. Henry was a little vague . . . was it ministry or business or philanthropy . . . ?"

Elliott was polite but not expansive. "Oh, I have done a lot of things, and different people probably think of me in very different ways," he replied. "But now, you are in ministry, and Henry says you are having a real problem in your parish. Please tell me about it."

And so Barry did tell, the whole story with its high hopes and unfulfilled promises and his feelings of betrayal by Jim and his strong dislike of the man, feelings that he fought because he knew that Christians, especially pastors, aren't supposed to dislike anyone, at least not as strongly as he disliked Jim. He was surprised by how much he opened up to Elliott, with a torrent of words, really. And he was surprised at just how deep his resentment was of Jim.

Elliott said almost nothing, not even acknowledging much of what Barry said, but it was clear that he was listening intently. Barry finally ran out of adrenaline and sank back in the couch, tired and sad and if anything even more depressed than before.

Elliott took several sips of his coffee, picked a piece of string off of his cardigan, got up, and adjusted the thermostat. Then he sat back down and fixed his eyes on Barry.

"Are you sure you are cut out to be a pastor?" Elliott asked in a clear, firm voice. Barry was too shocked to speak. "Because," Elliott continued, "I am not sure you have what it takes. It is a tough job, one of the toughest, and not all men and women are cut out for it.

"I really can't say much more or help you any until you have considered and answered that question," Elliott continued. "I am willing to meet with you again, but if you choose to come back, I suggest that you answer that basic question first. If not, we will be wasting each other's time and also wasting time you could be looking for a line of work that might fit you better."

Before he realized what was happening, Barry was being bundled into his coat by Elliott and shown the door. "Feel free to call, Barry," Elliott said as he shut the door, "but do some serious thinking first. That seems to have been the one thing you have *not* been doing."

Barely able to breathe, Barry stumbled down the long driveway toward his car. It wasn't until he had the key in the ignition and his seatbelt halfway on that the rage hit him.

CHAPTER 2
Ctrl + Alt + Delete = ?

enry was laughing so hard that Barry had to hold the phone several inches away from his ear. "Henry!" Barry cut in, "this is *so* not funny! It's not! I cannot believe you suggested I meet with a so-called friend of yours whose sole purpose seemed to be to question my calling to ministry and my significance as a human being! What kind of friend is this guy?"

It was a few more moments before Barry could make out Henry's words through the laughter. "Barry, this is great, this is so great! He got you too!"

"He got me? He *got* me? What in the world are you talking about?" asked Barry, tight-lipped and annoyed.

"I guess I should have warned you," said Henry, finally calming down, "but then you would have missed the effect of Elliott's style. He does this to everybody who's facing big life questions. He asks a question or makes a charge that is designed to shatter your assumptions, cause you to look at things from an entirely different perspective, and make you think really hard. He calls this a 'reframe,' and it really works. You just got the Elliott treatment, my man!"

"He didn't make me think," said Barry. "He just attacked me and put me on the defensive."

"Are you so sure?" Henry replied. "I bet you had never considered the possibility that ministry might not be the right deal for you. Am I right?"

Barry was silent for a few seconds because he couldn't think of a rejoinder. "Yeah, I guess that is right. But what purpose does that serve, other than to cause me to reach for a bottle of Scotch, when I don't even like Scotch?"

"Again, it's all about thinking," said Henry, quite serious now. "He takes you down to your core, to the very questions that are most important about life and yourself, and makes you wrestle with them.

He doesn't let you wade in the shallow end. He wants you in the deep water at the other end of the pool."

Barry was listening now, and Henry continued, "Look, you have to go see him again, as hard as that may seem. I know the guy well enough to know that he wants you to. He wouldn't give the Elliott treatment to someone if he didn't think there was something to them. He only challenges those he knows can take it and grow from it."

"I'm not so sure you're right," said Barry. "The old guy seemed a little too gleefully malicious to me. But I'll call him, I'll call him."

"I HAVE TO ADMIT THAT OUR FIRST conversation really threw me off, Elliott," said Barry, sinking back again into the couch in the older man's study. "I was angry at you and still am a little irritated and think you could have gone about things a different way. But Henry tells me that this is just something you do to help people like me."

"Some of my friends call it the Elliott treatment," said Elliott, smiling. "But I assure you that it is not a trick or a gimmick, and my question is in dead earnest. There is no more important question in life to ask than whether you are where you are meant to be, especially when it comes to one's vocation. So, Barry, have you thought through my question? Do you still believe that you are called to be a pastor?"

Barry was prepared for the question. "The short answer is yes, of course so. That's why I left a good-paying job and packed up my family for grad school and took this church. I still have a passion for serving God and others and want this to work. It's just that these struggles are so hard and frankly painful, and I'm not sure if I know what to do and how to do it." He paused for a moment, staring down at the rich carpet. "Can you help me?"

Elliott sat back in his chair and beamed, for the first time. "Barry, my friend, you have asked the right question! And you have done the right thing in admitting that you are powerless in your current situation. As my many friends in recovery would say, admitting you have a problem and can't fix it on your own is the first step to solving the problem."

Elliott stroked his right cheek with his fingertips and thought for a moment. "I want to be clear, though. I am not able to offer you any kind of quick fix. The fact is that the struggles you are facing with Jim Grendell and with others in the church have way more to do with you than with them. This is the first and in many ways the most important thing for you to grasp."

Barry started to protest, but Elliott continued, "And I know this is hard for you to hear and it may take a while for you to believe, and that's okay. Regardless of where the fault lies, these sorts of struggles in leadership are always rooted in the self, and in a combination of 'selfs' rubbing up against one another. When I said I could not offer quick fixes, this is what I had in mind. Real change takes courage, time, and energy. In many ways it is like a battle."

Elliott stood up and began to pace the room. "Quick-fix change does not work, because at its best it is no more than technical change—surface change designed to tinker with the nuts and bolts of a situation without altering its real dynamics. Technical change has its place, but it is not the ultimate answer. On the other hand, adaptive change has its roots inside of the self and represents a new way of thinking, perceiving, and, only then, behaving. Adaptive change involves values and underlying structures. You cannot have real change without an honest, deep look at yourself. It is precisely this fact—that change presupposes seeing things that can be uncomfortable and even frightening—that keeps most people on the level of technical, surface change and rules out deep and satisfying change.

"By the way, this applies not only to work but also to personal relationships."

"That's a lot to take in," Barry noted. "I feel like I need some time to absorb it, and I will, but I guess I also want to get to the heart of this. Assuming that I do take the deep look at myself you recommend and figure out my thoughts and motivations and all of that, then what do I *do*? My situation is pretty acute."

"As is everyone's," said Elliott with a smile. "Everyone feels that way, and believe me, Barry, I do not want to downplay the urgency of your dilemma or the realness of your pain. I am simply asking you to trust me for now, to be willing to dive into deeper water in the hope that at the other end of that process you will be better equipped to handle not only the Jim Grendell situation but others as well. Better yet, that you will know how to avoid similar landmines in the future."

Elliott stopped pacing, sat down, and looked into Barry's eyes. "I have to ask you something now. Do you want this? Do you want to understand not only your situation but also yourself better? Are you willing to dive into the deeper water?"

"Yes," Barry replied, his voice suddenly small. "I'm not sure what I will find there, but I have tried everything else and I think this is my last chance."

"Excellent," beamed Elliott for the second time. "Let's get started.

"As we move through this process of learning," Elliott began, "you will need to be patient. I am going to introduce a number of concepts to you, but that number will not be a terribly high one. What is most important is that you have a deep understanding of each one. So you will need to devote time and careful attention to reviewing each concept that we discuss, and also from time to time complete 'homework' assignments I will give you. Are you prepared to do this?"

Barry nodded, so Elliott continued. "As a matter of fact, we have touched on two of the most important concepts today. The first is that in conflict, the vast majority of the time, the problem is more in us than it is in the person with whom we are in conflict. So resolution does not come from winning or changing the behavior of the other person, but it begins with having the courage to look inside and ask probing questions of yourself.

"The second concept is related to the first. It is that technical change—change on the surface—is not lasting change. Real, lasting change is called adaptive change, change that alters the very structure of the relationship or environment and touches on the deepest of issues such as values.

"Now, these two concepts, which I understand you may or may not fully accept, play themselves out in a number of ways in the workplace or, as in your case, board-staff-congregation relationships. I want to give you an example. I call it the difference between living in the Red Zone and in the Blue Zone."

"I know all about the Red Zone," said Barry jokingly. "My favorite football team is totally incapable of scoring inside their opponents' twenty yard line!"

Elliott allowed himself a small smile and moved on. "I am a football fan too, but that's not what I'm talking about. One day I was working with a group which was caught up in all kinds of conflict and misunderstanding, and I was struggling to put words to what I was thinking. They had a large whiteboard in the room, kind of like this one." Elliott paused to open a cherry cabinet, revealing a whiteboard inside. "And there were only two markers—a red one and a blue one. I like to work with what I've got, so I started experimenting with the colors. Blue is the team color of my beloved alma mater, and so I chose that color to illustrate the good zone, the Blue Zone. And red is the color of my alma mater's most bitter rival, and so I chose that color to represent the negative Red Zone."

He paused and smiled at Barry and actually laughed out loud. "See, I told you I am a sports fan!"

Elliott rummaged in a desk drawer and pulled out both a red and a blue marker. "So I drew a line from top to bottom on the whiteboard." He did the same on his own whiteboard. "And I titled the left half 'Blue Zone' and the right half 'Red Zone' and wrote on each side in its corresponding color."

Elliott picked up the blue marker. "Now, the Blue Zone in the workplace is what we call Professional Mode, or the Emotional Cool Zone. There are several things that characterize this zone."

He scribbled a phrase on the left side of the board:

Focus on efficiency and effectiveness

"This is the sign of a high-functioning workplace. People are focused on the goals of the team, doing the right things, and doing them the right way. There is a certain feeling when a workplace is humming, when the people there feel like winners because they are doing their work well and smoothly."

Elliott moved down several inches on the whiteboard and wrote with the blue marker:

Structures of the organization are closely monitored and respected

"What this means," said Elliott, "is that expectations, performance goals, reporting relationships, agreed-upon standards, and the like are actually taken seriously. Job descriptions are held to, and performance evaluations are based on mutually agreed-upon standards and are not arbitrary. People are held accountable, but not in an overbearing way. Real accountability is related to trust; you cannot hold someone accountable if you do not trust them to live up to their end of the bargain to begin with. When standards shift and expectations change without negotiation, no one knows where they really stand, and this results in Red Zone reactions and behavior, which we will see in a minute."

Next, Elliott wrote:

Business issues are the first priority

"Now, Barry, this one is tough for people in the not-for-profit sector, particularly church leaders, a key part of whose business is caring for people. It is an easy and tempting thing to act as if caring for people includes not pointing out their failures to meet standards and performance expectations, and allowing their personal lives to disrupt their work performance and that of those around them. In fact, this has a devastating effect on both the employee and his or her colleagues."

Elliott cleared his throat and began to pace again. "Look, an organization that is focused on mission and has a clear set of core values and operating procedures is one that wins, one in which the employees have fun and are productive. But a workplace where one's personal agenda or problems detract from work, or where relational dramas and rivalries thicken the air, is an organization that underperforms and in which the workers are deeply unhappy.

"If the Blue Zone is where people are in professional mode and are emotionally cool, the Red Zone is where the atmosphere is characterized by a lack of professionalism and emotional heat, which can burn those who get too close.

"Are you starting to understand the Blue Zone a bit?" asked Elliott.

Barry squinted for a moment. "Yes, I think so. I understand the difference between technical and adaptive change, and I understand that an organization in which there is focus on results, consistent standards, and a constant commitment to the corporate mission is probably a really satisfying place to work. What I am not seeing clearly is how you can hold to these standards so tightly and still make the workplace, or a church board, a place where people are valued and cared for."

"That is a great observation, Barry," said Elliott. "Good job. Instead of answering that directly, I am going to go ahead and move through the Red Zone, okay?"

Barry nodded, so Elliott picked up the red marker and wrote on the right side of the board:

Focus more on feelings than results

"This is the opposite of a focus on efficiency and effectiveness," Elliott pointed out, waving his hand at the blue side of the whiteboard. "When we focus more on feelings and personal issues than on results, it creates uncertainty in the work environment. People are not sure where their personal and professional boundaries lie, and everyone is unsure about how to act. Inevitably this slows down the pace of a company and allows it to get derailed by issues that are not tied to the organizational mission."

"Like when Jim Grendell brings up how pastors get more time off than others," Barry said, "and when he brings up how personally 'disappointed' he is—"

"Perhaps," said Elliott. "But be careful, Barry. Remember that the focus in understanding these truths is on looking inside, not on pointing the finger at others. As a matter of fact, one of the classic traits of Red Zone behavior is blame-shifting, a lack of willingness to accept that one is part of the problem and not just a victim.

"Let me keep going, please, Barry. We are almost done. When we focus on feelings rather than results, we get caught up in conflict and we don't get our work done well, and so no one is happy. But when our corporate focus is on good work and on the common mission, the organization becomes a place of effectiveness and, dare I say it, fun!"

Before Barry could erupt at the thought of his job being fun, Elliott grabbed the red marker and wrote:

No common standards and no way of monitoring performance and behavior

"Again, this is the flip side of Blue Zone behavior. In the Red Zone, no one knows where they stand, what is expected of them, what is appropriate and inappropriate, and even whether they are doing a good job. That creates tons of uncertainty and anxiety. And when people get uncertain and anxious, they generally don't know how to handle that, and the easy thing is to lash out at others as the cause of one's anxiety. Get a group of people doing that and lapsing into cycles of anxiety, anger, blame, recrimination ... well, you get the picture.

"One more thing, and then we are done for today." Elliott wrote across the bottom righthand side of the whiteboard, again with red ink:

People expect the organization to be a family and they assume family roles

When he finished writing, the whiteboard looked like this:

Blue Zone	Red Zone
Focus on efficiency and effectiveness	Focus more on feelings than results
Structures of the organization are closely monitored and respected	No common standards and no way of monitoring performance and behavior
Business issues are the first priority	People expect the organization to be a family and they assume family roles

"Now, this is one for you to really dwell on, Barry," said Elliott. "A lot of folks expect and even want their church to be like a family.

And indeed, there are some familial aspects to a church; people are expected to take care of each other and be involved in each other's lives more than in a secular organization. But when it comes to the leadership function of a church, expecting family behavior is a recipe for disaster."

"Okay, I have tracked with everything so far," interrupted Barry, "but I have a hard time here. Churches are *not* businesses, as my seminary professors reminded me again and again. Sure, they are organizations, but they cannot have the hard-core, competitive, every person for themselves edge that corporations do. The church has to be different. I don't know if you read the Bible much, but Jesus said that the church is to be set apart, different from the world."

"I do not dispute your theology, Barry," said Elliott, a little sternly. "But I do want to challenge your assumptions. Now, who said that a business had to be hard core, competitive, cutthroat? There are many more Christian business people than there are pastors. Do you really think Jesus wanted all of them to be nice and gracious at church but then competitive, cutthroat monsters at work?"

Barry could not think of a thing to say.

"It's a rhetorical question, clearly," said Elliott, a little more softly. "My point is not that a church is to try to be like a business in every way. My point is that the church and a business have one crucial thing in common: they are both organizations composed of people.

"And another thing: neither one is a family. Hang on, Barry.

"Families are critically important, but they are different from work organizations. Families are designed to nurture, train, discipline, and orient their members to face the outside world with one constant—each other, relationships that are intended to survive no matter what. The same can't be said of organizations.

"In organizations, people often have to make choices—sometimes choices to leave the organization—due to family responsibilities. A healthy person subordinates her work to the needs of her family and draws a clear boundary between the two. It is when the two get confused that conflict and misunderstanding and anxiety emerge. There are things that families can do that organizations, even churches, cannot. Workplaces and families both serve critical but very different purposes. A healthy organization is full of people who understand this and give their all to family (or other critical relationships, for those without family) and also give their all to the organization, but in very different ways."

Elliott paused and smiled. "I can see by the fact that you are massaging your temples that we have probably hit overload for the day, so let me sum up and give you an assignment, if I may.

"Bottom line, when an organization operates in the Blue Zone, the members operate on a healthy, professional level, with clear expectations and standards of behavior. But in the Red Zone, people allow their behavior to be driven by personal, emotional, and unprofessional motives. Often this shows up in petty conflict, jealousy, cutthroat behavior, and inconsistent performance. Working in the Blue Zone is fun, challenging, and rewarding. Working in the Red Zone is, well, you know, don't you Barry?"

Barry nodded. "This is so much to take in. I feel like a guy drinking from a fire hydrant."

"Right," replied Elliott. "And so I want to leave you with an assignment or two. When you get back to your home or office, open your journal or boot up your computer and write down the things we have talked about today. Then, every day for the next week, review what you have written. But don't just read it for content, Barry. The step I want you to take involves an inward look. Ask yourself questions such as these:

- "Am I more of a Red Zone or a Blue Zone leader?
- "What are examples of Red Zone and Blue Zone behavior that I have demonstrated this week?
- "Do I tend to focus more on technical or adaptive change when I meet an obstacle?

"And then write about these things too."

As Barry prepared to leave, he paused at Elliott's formidable front door. "Thanks. I will call again in a couple of weeks, and I will do the assignments you have given me. I have to say I felt more comfortable with you this time. It's good to know that you can actually laugh!"

Elliott's eyes twinkled, just barely. "Oh, people are often surprised by how often I do laugh. I am honestly the most joyous man you are likely to know," he said as he shook Barry's hand and closed the front door.

As Barry reached the bottom of the stoop, the door swung open again and Barry turned around to see Elliott's face. "One more thing, Barry. I am glad you have seen me laugh, but I would not advise you to get too comfortable with me. You have barely begun to dip your big toe in the deep water. I will look forward to your call. Goodbye."

Barry had the drive home to wonder whether Elliott had been serious.

CHAPTER 3

It's All about You

Barry had about half an hour before he needed to leave for Elliott's house, so he decided to swing by home first and say hi to Sophia and his kids. He pulled into his garage and was wiping his feet on the mat inside the mudroom when he heard Sophia and one of his children speaking in tones more intense than normal.

He stepped into the kitchen, and his sixteen-year-old son, Jake, looked up at Barry as if his dad had caught him doing something wrong. "Hi, Dad," Jake mumbled and brushed past Barry and out the door without meeting his father's eyes.

"What's up with him?" Barry asked Sophia after Jake had pulled out of the garage in his old Taurus.

Sophia didn't seem to want to meet Barry's eyes either, but in a moment she looked up. "Aren't you heading over to your friend Elliott's? Maybe I should wait to fill you in until you get back."

"Sophia, you know I can never wait when you say something like that," Barry sighed, leaning against the kitchen counter. "Go ahead, fill me in."

"It's his midquarter report card," said Sophia.

"You mean . . ." Barry began.

"Right, not good," Sophia finished. "Neither English nor history is better, and biology is actually worse. His biology teacher is saying that she doesn't understand how a kid as bright as Jake can continue to come in unprepared for class assignments and labs."

Barry felt a familiar sinking feeling in his stomach. He turned his back on Sophia, hesitated a moment, and smacked his palm against the laminate countertop. "What is *up* with that kid?" he exploded, smacking the counter again. "How many times do we have to warn him to work harder, to be more serious and committed? What do we have to do? We've grounded him, checked his homework like a third

grader's parents, bribed him ... the stubborn kid just doesn't get it!"
He paused and Sophia just looked at him.

"Well, this time I know what I'm going to do," said Barry, strid-
ing across the kitchen toward the refrigerator. "When he gets back
from wherever he just went, I am taking the keys to that car and he
is going to be stuck here where he will have plenty of time to get his
act together, that's what I'm going to do. One way or another, he is
going to get his grades up!" Barry popped the top on a Diet Coke,
took a too-deep gulp, and looked at Sophia with a determined glare,
trying not to cough as the carbonated soda found its way to the back
of his throat.

"Are you finished yet?" asked Sophia, with a half-smile on her
face. "Before we start refitting the basement as a torture chamber for
Jake, maybe we should think through this a bit first and try to figure out what is really going on."

"Look, honey," replied Barry, "we know what is going on. Jake is
slacking off in his homework and commitment to his classes. And
we know what's going to happen. His grades really are starting to
matter for college admissions, and if he doesn't watch out, he won't
be able to get into any college at all."

"Barry, I know this is serious. But let's not lose perspective. The
fact is that what we've tried so far—punishment, grounding, badg-
ering—hasn't worked. Maybe we should try a different strategy."

Unable to contain himself, Barry cut Sophia off. "Why should
we change? It's Jake that needs to change. He just needs to apply
himself, work harder, stop defying us and his teachers, or he's not
going to be able to get into college, which you and I both know will
put a severe monkey wrench in his future success!

"Look," Barry continued, "I am not going to let that happen. That
is not going to happen to Jake and to us. He is smart enough to make
good grades, and he will. When I was his age, I played sports just
like he does and I still got good grades! Maybe the problem is that
band he's in. We'll have to take that away along with the car. I will
do whatever it takes."

Barry turned away in disgust and muttered, "I'm sick of hearing
those drums banging in the basement all night anyway, and the howl-

ing of that electric guitar. Come to think of it, the basement already sounds as if there is a torture chamber down there!"

Sophia dried her hands on a dishtowel and threaded the towel through the refrigerator door handle. "Barry, I am as frustrated as you are. I don't know why Jake isn't working harder to get his grades up. You and I both know that he is a smart kid. I want him to do better too. But I don't think further punishment and pressure is going to help, because it hasn't been working so far."

"You're wrong, Sophia," Barry replied. "The fact of the matter is that I, I mean we, haven't been firm enough. If we had been more firm at the outset, we could have gotten Jake back on the right track before all of this started spinning out of control. But I've learned my lesson. Jake is going to start trying harder and doing better, and I will be as resolved and firm as I have to be to make sure of it."

"No matter what, right, Barry?" asked Sophia. "No matter the consequences or long-term effects?"

"Don't put words in my mouth, Sophia. You know what I mean. I'm not trying to dictate Jake's life, but I am going to make sure that while he is in my house, he is going to meet certain standards, and one of those is effort in school. I'm not trying to be a tyrant, but I am trying to protect our values as a family, which is bigger than any one person."

There was a silence of a few moments as Sophia weighed her next words carefully.

"Barry, I am going to say something that may be hard for you to hear, but I think I need to say it. You know how you talk about Jim Grendell, how in the church he is ruthless about his goals and ideas, how nothing can get in his way?"

"Sophia, what does Jim Grendell have to do with this? That's the church, this is the fam—"

"Honey, let me finish," Sophia interjected. "I know how frustrating dealing with Jim is for you, how his stubbornness makes you so mad, and how you feel like he is more than willing to steamroll anyone and anything in his path."

"Right, but I still don't see what this has to do with—"

"Barry, what I am trying to tell you is that sometimes I feel the way with you that you feel with Jim. I feel like sometimes you are inflexible and that you will take no prisoners in making sure every-thing turns out the way you want it to turn out."

Barry took a step back as if Sophia had slapped him. His face turned red, and to his surprise he felt tears spring up in his eyes. Angry tears.

"You can't mean, how can you say . . ." he sputtered.

Pausing a second and aligning his words more carefully, he continued. "You know the real problem here, Sophia? The problem is that you are too easy on Jake. You have always been too easy on the kids. And maybe even a deeper problem is that you don't support me when I am trying to give the kids discipline and structure and tough love. You want to know what's really wrong? It's that we are not consistent with Jake. We send him two different messages, you and I. And the message you send him undercuts my message and is frankly the biggest reason why we find ourselves in this mess with Jake."

Snatching his keys off of the kitchen counter, Barry headed out the mudroom door to his car. Just before leaving, he turned around once more. "Sophia, the problem is not that I'm like Jim Grendell. God knows, I have my faults, but being like that man is not one of them. If you want to know the problem, you better take a look at the way you coddle Jake and fail to support me." Barry spoke this final sentence slowly, pausing after each word for emphasis.

"And one more thing, Sophia, comparing me to Jim Grendell is the cheapest shot you have ever thrown my way."

And then Barry was gone.

FOR HALF OF THE TRIP TO ELLIOTT'S HOUSE, Barry replayed his conversation with Sophia in his head, unconsciously speaking out loud. Then he caught himself and fell silent, spending the remaining fifteen minutes in the car seething in silence at the unfairness of Sophia's ambush.

Seconds after Elliott had opened his front door, he touched Barry's shoulder for a split second. "Rough day at the office, Barry?" he asked.

"No, the office was fine, Elliott," said Barry, moving quickly from the foyer to the sanctuary of the brown couch in Elliott's study, on which he fell heavily. "The problem was home, when I stopped by for a few minutes before coming out here."

"What happened?" Elliott asked.

"It's Jake's grades again," said Barry. "The kid just won't improve his effort in school. And now this is coming between Sophia and me. I don't know why she won't support me in holding Jake accountable.

"You know what, Elliott? She actually compared me to Jim Grendell. She said I act at home like he acts at church. Can you believe that?"

Barry's question wasn't really in search of an answer, so Elliott remained silent for a long moment while Barry tried to get his breathing under control.

"Do you want to talk about it, Barry?" Elliott asked finally.

"You know what, no, Elliott. I don't have the energy. But thanks. Anyway it doesn't have anything to do with what we have been talking about." Barry sat up and fished a legal pad from his briefcase.

"I've got the assignment you gave me, keeping track of the ways in which I behave as a Red Zone leader and as a Blue Zone leader."

"Okay," Elliott said, with a hesitance that Barry didn't catch. "Let's talk about that then."

Barry flipped over the top page of his legal pad. "To be honest, I couldn't really list a lot of Blue Zone behaviors. Basically, I really do love and serve the people on the staff and in the congregation. I try to encourage them, and I spent some time this week with Stephanie, our youth ministry intern, who is a really needy young woman with a lot of emotional problems who looks at me as some kind of father figure. I'm not sure she should even be in seminary or interning at the church, but I really tried to be patient and empathetic with her, even though it really cut into my time."

Barry looked up from the paper and glanced at Elliott, who nodded at him to continue.

"In the board meeting last Monday, Jim Grendell and a couple of his cronies were harping about something totally off the agenda, and I tried really hard not to let it get to me and to keep from Red Zoning, and I mostly succeeded.

"You asked me to take note of Red Zone behaviors as well, and I did find some. I got really upset when the small groups coordinator didn't get me the recent reports on numbers in the small groups on time. I needed those numbers for planning and budgeting purposes, but I still probably overreacted. But I think mostly because the small groups coordinator is just not doing a very good job.

"And when I came back from my meeting with the youth intern, distracted and with a pile of work to do, I snapped at my assistant. I guess I was taking out my frustration on her a little bit."

Barry fell silent and gave Elliott space to ask a question. "How about at home, Barry? Did you find examples of Red Zone and Blue Zone behavior there?"

"I know you said to look for that," Barry replied. "But the principles seemed to apply more to work than to home. The behaviors seemed easier to spot there, and I didn't have a lot of emotional energy to work on translating the Red Zone, Blue Zone concepts into my family life."

"Is that pretty much what you came up with, Barry?" asked Elliott. Barry nodded and Elliott leaned back in his leather wingback chair and sat in silence for enough time that Barry began to grow uncomfortable.

Just as Barry was about to break the silence, Elliott leaned forward. "Barry, first let me say that I am glad you had the guts to tackle the assignment. Not everyone is willing to go that far, to put their ankles into the deep water. But you did, and I commend you for that."

Before Barry had time to feel pleased with himself, Elliott continued. "That said, Barry, I find that your examples have a couple of common themes.

"The first is that they are superficial. They did not even begin to scratch the surface. To your credit, you have begun to grasp the difference between life in the Red Zone and life in the Blue Zone, but I had hoped your understanding would be a bit deeper.

"Of course, that's my fault," Elliott added quickly. "I should have done a better job anchoring those concepts in your mind and heart.

"The second thing I noticed is that every single instance of Red Zone behavior you saw in yourself was someone else's fault, at least in your telling of the story."

Barry sat upright in indignation. "Elliott, you have to be kidding me! I made it as clear as I could that they were my fault. I snapped at my assistant after an emotionally draining meeting, I overreacted to the small groups coordinator's lateness in turning in the report . . . those were my fault."

Elliott wouldn't be deterred. "Right, Barry, but in each instance you tied your Red Zone behavior to someone else's actions. You snapped at your assistant because you had a draining meeting, you snapped at the small groups coordinator because the report was late, and you snapped at Sophia because she was not as supportive of you in the discipline of Jake as you thought she should have been."

"How do you mix Sophia in with the other two?" Barry asked, with a puzzled expression on his face.

"Simply because the Red Zone principles are the same both at home and at work, no matter the context," Elliott answered. "Red Zone behavior has its start in the person who demonstrates the behavior, not in external circumstances. If you are living in the Red Zone, you can expect Red Zone behavior to emerge at the slightest provocation. If you are living in the Blue Zone, you tend to react in a Blue Zone way regardless of external circumstances. The zones are something you carry inside of you."

Barry was thoughtful, silent, so Elliott continued. "Barry, at the outset I told you that you would have to be willing to dive into deep water if you want to understand why the challenges in your life are creating such stress and anxiety. If you will remember, at our last meeting, I told you that the sorts of struggles you were having at the church with Jim were really struggles rooted in yourself. To dive into the deep water of self-understanding and living in the Blue Zone, it is critical that you accept that conflict is always more about us than it is about the other person."

"I know you said that, Elliott," responded Barry. "And I try to remind myself of that. But it is tricky to keep track of. And sometimes it seems a stretch. If what you're saying is right, then even my argument with Sophia today had more to do with me than with her. It even had more to do with me than with the situation, or with Jake. Is that really what you are asking me to believe?"

Elliott simply sat in his chair, silent, but with a penetrating gaze. "Okay, okay," said Barry, breaking the stare by looking away. "You are saying that, I know. But if that is true, what hope do I have? Do I just have to blame myself for every conflict regardless of how right my point of view may be?"

"Barry, blame is a word we must banish from our discussion of these things," said Elliott with arresting force. "Because if we blame others, we are able to avoid the hard work of taking a look inside, where real change can occur. And if we blame ourselves, we usually fall into a cycle of self-recrimination and guilt which equally prevents real change. These things are not a matter of blame but are a matter of understanding, which leads to change. There is all the difference in the world between those two things."

Elliott stood up and motioned Barry toward the door. "Barry, forgive me, but I have another meeting and I need to prepare for that, but I want to mention one more thing as you are leaving." The two men walked into the foyer.

"What I want to say is that you have a very wise wife in Sophia, and that you should listen well to her. She said that she sometimes experiences you as you experience Jim Grendell, and there is much food for thought there. Your assignment for next time is simply to think about that and ask yourself how that could be, since you detest Jim's behavior so much."

Elliott put his hand on the doorknob to let Barry out, and Barry paused as he started through the door. "That's a tough one, Elliott. I'm not really sure how to begin to answer that, even how to get started thinking about that. Do you have any ideas?"

Elliott smiled just a little. "I do, actually. You might start by meditating on the fact that every time I hear you talk about Jim Grendell, I hear you talking about yourself." Elliott waved and shut the front door.

Barry stood alone on the steps. *Why does he end our meetings like that every time?* he wondered and turned to begin the long drive home.

CHAPTER 4

Things Fall Apart

Barry had less time than he would have liked to reflect seriously on Elliott's parting statement. There was a meeting of the church board that evening, and Barry knew that he would have to be razor sharp in order to lead the board well through what promised to be a contentious discussion.

When Barry was being recruited to come to First Community, the selection committee made it clear that the most important job of the new pastor was to reach out to the increasing numbers of young families moving into the neighborhoods surrounding the church. During his installation service, Jim Grendell, the head of the committee, reminded Barry in the presence of the congregation of this charge.

"Barry, we have called you here to be the pastor and shepherd to this congregation, but we have also called you so that you can help us reach out to those around us who are not committed to any church. Your youth and energy will help you in this challenge, and the people of this congregation stand ready to do our part to support you."

Barry had been advised to move slowly in making broad changes in the church's ministry. He reasoned that even though the congregation wanted change, change was still a hard thing, and that the people might not fully realize the depth of change that would be required of them in order to reach an entirely different demographic group.

So in his first year as pastor, Barry had concentrated on investing in the lives of the congregation and its leaders and working to understand the history, traditions, and habits of the church. The only changes he made were small ones, such as spending a little extra money to brighten the children's ministry rooms and adding to his sermons an occasional illustration designed to be relevant to the parents of young children, although there were not terribly many in his audience. In addition, Barry and Sophia had committed to getting to know their neighbors, their lives and children, in hopes that over time some of their new friends would indicate spiritual interest or a desire to see their own children involved in a church.

In his second year, Barry had decided to make slightly bolder changes, such as introducing contemporary instruments into the worship service and offering praise music in addition to the traditional hymns the congregation was used to. He heard a few grumbles from older members of the church who suggested that the new songs weren't quite reverent enough or that the new instruments were too loud, but by and large the congregation did not seem to object.

Even more significant, two neighboring families of the Wolf's, the Wilson and Davis families, began to attend First Community. Barry and Sophia had enjoyed cookouts with the families, Barry had been to a couple of Cubs games with Rick Wilson and Todd Davis, their kids seemed to enjoy hanging out, and they began to form close friendships.

As the three couples grew closer, both the Wilsons and Davises casually asked if they could come to the church, once, just to "check out what Barry was up to on Sunday mornings." Barry and Sophia were delighted, and they were positively thrilled when the couples began to attend regularly. The Wilsons in particular became involved quickly, as Sandra agreed to take the reins of a new youth ministry and Rick volunteered to oversee the church's finance committee.

Most of the long-time members of the church welcomed the new couples and several of the couples' friends who had also been attending the church. Barry was encouraged that he was realizing success in carrying out the charge the selection committee had given him. He was convinced that First Community was nearing a tipping point when young families would begin to come to the church in numbers.

With that in mind, Barry began to make changes in the church designed to make it attractive to the families Barry predicted would be coming soon.

The church completed the renovation of the children's wing. They spruced up the basketball area out back, replacing the weathered goalpost and drooping, netless rim with a sleek glass-backboard model. Volunteer crews trimmed the weeds around the little-used softball field and rechalked the lines, and the church formed its first team in ages.

Perhaps most important, Barry had begun (finally, in his mind) to modernize elements of the worship service. He stopped putting outlines in the worship bulletin and began to project the main points of his sermons via PowerPoint onto a newly installed screen. Contemporary praise songs pushed traditional hymns almost completely off the service agenda.

Barry began to show clips of recent films to illustrate points in his messages. And he moved from a verse-by-verse teaching of Bible books to a more thematic approach. His goal was to apply the Bible to the day-to-day lives of young families, and the names of his sermon series began to transition from titles such as "The Joy of Redemption" to "Biblical Principles for Strong Families" and "How to Raise Great Kids in Dangerous Times."

With each transition, Barry heard a few more grumbles, but the protests seemed to be under control, and Barry ascribed them to inevitable growing pains.

On this afternoon, Barry sat in his office going over his notes for the evening board meeting. Tonight was to be the regular six-month review of ministries and finances in which the board weighed in on the everyday life of the church. During his time at First Community, Barry had largely succeeded at changing the tone of these meetings from petty criticisms of details to a strategy session in which the board evaluated the previous six months in light of the church's mission statement.

But this afternoon Barry was worried. Sophia and Barry had both heard whisperings that tonight was going to be a showdown. Jim Grendell, who would chair the meeting, had not returned Barry's calls for three days, in spite of the fact that Barry had seen Jim's car parked next to his warehouse across the street from the church. And perhaps most ominous, Jim had not submitted to Barry an agenda for the meeting, departing from routine.

Barry breathed a quick prayer, straightened the papers on his desk, grabbed his legal pad and pen, and walked down the hall to the board's conference room. *It would be nice to have Elliott here to help me through this meeting,* he thought as he eased into his chair at the conference table.

Precisely at 7:00 p.m., Jim called the meeting to order. After an opening prayer, Jim turned to Barry. "Pastor, I'm sorry I didn't have an agenda for you prior to tonight's meeting. To be honest, the agenda has changed in the last few days. A number of members of the board have suggested that we have more than our usual perfunctory review tonight. What these board members believe is that we should have a very serious discussion about the whole philosophy of our church and how it seems to be drifting in some dangerous directions.

"I am merely representing other members of the board," Jim continued. "But I bow to the wishes of these godly men and women. It is important that we have this discussion, and the forum tonight, Pastor, will allow for us to have some straight talk and to ask you some pointed questions. I am sure you will agree that it is much better for us to deal with this out in the open than to pretend the issues are not there, correct?"

Barry felt trapped and nervous, but he couldn't figure out how to challenge Jim's question. He merely nodded his head.

"Barry, I have tried to summarize the comments I have heard, and they seem to fall into several categories."

Jim looked down at his notes. "First, there is a theological concern. A lot of people feel that you are watering down your theology by moving away from the Bible and on to pop culture references which have no place in church.

"There is also a pastoral concern. We all want to reach the young families in our area, but we have to take care of the people we already have too. We have seniors here who have a lot of needs and a lot of faithful people who are used to good strong Bible teaching, and their needs have to be met as well.

"A lot of people have financial concerns too," Jim continued. "We have spent an awful lot of money on superficial, cosmetic things like a basketball court and a softball field, and some people feel that we are wasting God's money. And there is a lot of concern over the big screen in the sanctuary. It just doesn't seem to fit, and when you can always put your sermon notes in the bulletin, we're not sure why the expense for the screen and projector was necessary."

Barry noted that for the first time Jim had referred to himself as sharing the feelings of the nameless others whose opinions he claimed to represent.

"We've noticed that a lot of these financial decisions have come since your friend Rick Wilson has taken the reins of the financial committee," said Jim. "And there is some concern as well that you and some of the newer members of the church are trying to grab the power here. I know you are probably not really trying to do that, but perception is everything, and right now that's the way it looks.

"And I guess that leads me to the last concern," Jim said, swiveling in his chair and looking at Barry directly for the first time in the meeting. "All of these other issues seem to point to an overall leadership issue. We know that you are well intentioned, but you are pretty green at being a pastor. This is your first pastorate, and you haven't had the years of experience and seasoning to learn that you just can't make changes at this fast of a pace and while alienating a lot of sincere, mature Christian people.

"It is a tough job, and we are willing to see if you can do it after all." Jim's gaze took in the entire room of board members. "But we want to save this church, not see it split apart into pieces because of a pastor's well-intentioned but not really great leadership."

Bizarrely, Jim put his hand tenderly on Barry's right shoulder. "Barry, you know I have a great deal of fondness for you in my heart." Barry noticed with a strange sense of detachment that Jim's eyes were teary and his voice was quavering a little. "But I'm not sure if you are up to this, and I don't want to see either you or the church get hurt as a result."

There was a long and very uncomfortable silence as Jim ended his presentation. Barry glanced around the room and noticed that two or three board members were glaring at him, while the majority of the others looked profoundly uncomfortable and had a hard time meeting Barry's gaze. All seemed to be waiting on someone to say something, and Barry sensed it was time for him to step up.

"I think I hear you, Jim," he began in a voice that was surprisingly level. "You don't think I'm measuring up as a preacher, financial leader, pastor, or leader. That's quite a resume of failure. You have blindsided and manipulated me by not sharing your thoughts prior to this meeting, and I don't appreciate that. But at the same time I do not want to hurt the church. If I am that kind of failure, it may indeed be time to make a switch. I don't really feel comfortable talking about that now, since this is Jim's meeting, but I do think it would be best for me to leave so that you all may talk about these very important matters."

With that, Barry got up and left the room.

BARRY AND ELLIOTT HAD NEVER MET at night, but Elliott had agreed quickly to make some time when Barry had called from the cell phone in his car immediately after leaving the board meeting. Barry had described the meeting very briefly, and Elliott had invited him to come out to the house right away.

At night, Elliott's stately house was beautiful, framed by the tall trees and the moonlight. As Elliott opened the door, it occurred to Barry that he had never seen or heard anyone else in the house. He made a mental note to ask Elliott about that sometime.

Elliott, impeccably dressed as always, invited Barry into his study and onto the now-familiar brown couch. He listened as Barry replayed the board meeting. When Barry was done, Elliott gave a low whistle through his teeth.

"That sounds like a nightmare of a meeting, Barry," Elliott said, leaning back in his chair. "Yet you seem calmer than you might have been weeks ago. What are you feeling and thinking?"

"I should be angry, I suppose," replied Barry. "And I am, at some level. But mostly I feel numb. And resigned. Maybe you were right the very first time we met when you said I might not be up to this job. I spent the drive out here thinking about where we would move, what I would do to support Sophia and the kids if I left this pastorate."

"I can certainly understand how you might be feeling that way, Barry," said Elliott. "It's not easy for any man to have his character and competency questioned, especially in front of others and in a forum in which he is not free to defend himself. Let me ask you this, though. Is there a part of you that wants to do something other than to run away?"

Barry thought for a moment and a fierce light seemed to come into his eyes. He stood up suddenly. "You know what, there is, Elliott!" he exclaimed. "And I actually think that that part of me is bigger than the one that wants to flee and protect. What I really want to do is to take the fight right back at Jim Grendell, to show him and those weak people whom he has manipulated that he can't get away with that behavior. You know, I bet Jim has been doing this his whole life, bullying people who stand in his way. Someone has to stop it, and that someone might as well be me. I am the pastor after all, and if a pastor can't be strong in a church, who is going to be?"

Barry sat back down on the couch, only this time his posture was not a slump but instead was ramrod straight. "What do you think, Elliott?"

Elliott put his thumb under his chin and his index finger on his mouth and considered Barry for a moment. "I think, Barry, that we are getting close to something very important here.

"One consistent theme in our conversations has been your deep dislike for Jim and the things you perceive he has done to undermine you and your leadership. And he has in fact done some of those things. There can be no doubt about that."

Elliott stood up, walked over to one of the large windows in his study, and looked outside, his back facing Barry. "Yes," he said after a moment, "I do think we are getting somewhere."

Elliott turned around and came and sat on the opposite end of the couch. "So let's not let this moment pass, my friend," he said.

"Tell me, Barry, what is it about Jim that disturbs you the most, that causes you to react so strongly to him? I'm speaking not so much of his actions as of his character traits."

Barry answered quickly, "He's a know-it-all. He plays power games to make himself feel important. His own power is more important to him than the welfare of the church. And all of this comes from his own insecurity and fear that his life has been a failure. He is fake and hides his true identity. I hate that last thing most of all, his insincerity and phoniness. The Jim that he shows the world is nothing like the real Jim, the man he is inside.

"And the irony of the whole thing is that as a man, he doesn't really have the track record or the platform to claim the kind of great success or competence that leads to superior leadership and the right to tell others what to do. He has been a modestly successful businessman. But most of his wealth was from his wife's family ... he married into money. He did fine in insurance, I guess, but now he just owns a few properties, like that run-down, dismal warehouse across the street from my office. It looked fine a few years ago, and trucks were coming and going, but now it sits mostly empty, gathering cobwebs.

"Maybe that warehouse is a metaphor for the man. I've never thought of that before," said Barry. "His image looks good on the outside, but on the inside there is nothing there. I do think I despise that most of all, the fact that the inside does not match the outside."

Barry paused, seemingly struck by this new realization, giving Elliott a chance to respond.

"Barry," said the older man, "have you ever met Jim Grendell before?"

"Met him before?" responded Barry. "What do you mean? The first time I met him was when his committee began to recruit me to come to First Community."

Elliott smiled a wisp of a smile. "I didn't mean have you met Jim Grendell the man before. I meant, have you ever met anyone like him, with those traits which annoy you so much?"

Barry wrinkled his forehead in thought. "I don't know, but I do know this. The traits Jim has, the ones that I described, have always driven me crazy. I have to pray for patience when I come across someone who is a bully or a know-it-all or pretends to be something they aren't or who tries to impress others beyond what they really have to offer."

Elliott smiled, again a wisp. "Okay, Barry. Now we're down to the heart of it." Elliott got up from the couch and walked over to the cherry cabinet containing his whiteboard. He swung the doors open and then unbuttoned the cuffs of his crisp blue button-down shirt, rolling them up twice. He found a green marker and wrote a sentence on the whiteboard:

We meet the same person over and over again

Elliott turned around and noticed Barry's face crinkled in confusion. "Wondering what I mean?" he chuckled. Barry nodded.

"All of us have people in our lives that elicit strong emotions," said Elliott. "Now that is a truly unfortunate phrase, but you understand what I'm saying. In particular, there are certain traits that show up in other people that drive us to distraction. For some people that is lateness or laziness, for others disrespect or a foul mouth, for still others bragging or acting superior. And the list goes on. Are you with me so far?"

"Sure," Barry replied. "Keep going."

"The problem is that these traits that have power for us are traits that reside within us. We're not aware of these traits because we don't like them, and when we see them in others, we automatically react."

Elliott picked up the marker, turned to the board, but then turned back to Barry. "Let's put those two things together. Can you see it?"

Barry nodded. "I think so. You're saying that all of us have a list of traits which annoy us and that some of these traits, for whatever reason, actually lead us to be angry and avoidant and sometimes even hostile toward people who demonstrate them."

"Exactly right, Barry," beamed Elliott. Turning back to the whiteboard again, he continued. "A minute ago I wrote that we keep meeting the same person over and over—that person who has traits we cannot stand. You understand that. Now let me finish that thought for you."

Elliott wrote a second sentence underneath the first:

And that person is you

Elliott put an emphatic green underline to his phrase and turned around to see a truly confused Barry.

"Elliott, you had me. And now you've lost me. What do you mean?"

"I'm glad you asked that," replied Elliott with a wide smile. "Let's get into the deep water now. When we react to traits in someone else, it is important to understand that we are really reacting to something inside ourselves. You are a pastor, so can I try to put it into mildly theological language for you?"

Barry nodded.

"Barry, the fundamental fact of human nature is that we are all of us complex beings having both a part that we readily acknowledge and embrace—our aware side—and a side that is denied—our unaware side. The aware side is that part of us we really like, that is cheerful, hopeful, kind, concerned for the welfare of others, committed to our faith, brave . . . you understand my point.

"That other side, that we are not aware of, tends to get denied and pushed away. But you can't deny a part of yourself. When you do, it comes out in other ways, usually destructive ones."

Elliott fell into his familiar leather chair and raked his right hand through his thick white hair. Barry noticed that the lines in Elliott's face seemed deepened, as if this conversation was costing him something. Elliott seemed tired. And yet he seemed fully alive. It was that look in his eyes. Not a twinkle, exactly, but more like a reflection of some fire burning deep inside the man.

"When we discover the part of us we don't like, that is the moment we can learn the most about ourselves. That will also allow us to help others as well. It's not the part of us we know but the part of us we don't know that will be the most beneficial."

Elliott looked up again, directly at Barry. "I know it has been a long and hard night for you, Barry. But I feel that I need to bring a few strands together from our discussion. Do you have a few more minutes?"

Barry agreed, so Elliott continued. "I said two things earlier. First, we keep meeting the same person over and over again in our lives— the person with the traits which are most repugnant to us and sometimes cause a violent reaction in us. Second, I said that the person you keep meeting again and again is you. Let me clarify that and tie it together with the denied and acknowledged sides of who we are.

"When we react so strongly and negatively to traits in another person, it is a certain indication that we are actually reacting to something that is lodged in our unaware side. Those traits in that person remind us of something in ourselves, or something we fear could be in ourselves. If we have not acknowledged and begun to understand our denied side, then we cannot deal with the fact that these things are in us. It is simply too threatening. So we have to do something with that angst.

"What we do with this angst is to see it in other people. And we project it onto the person against whom we react so strongly. They become a movie screen onto which we project our own selves. It is easier to look at these things when they are outside of us and easier to deny the pain of them when we can attach them to someone else. You are doing this with Jim. He is your movie screen."

Barry felt agitated and began to shift uncomfortably in his seat.

"Barry, you have not yet understood your own denied side, your own capacity to be and to do what you see in Jim. Jim represents that part of you that you fear the most. His insecurities are actually your insecurities. It's just easier to see them in someone else than in yourself. When you react with loathing toward Jim, then you are really expressing a loathing of yourself."

Barry felt like he was about to explode, and Elliott sensed it.

"Just a few more thoughts, Barry. Jesus once said to people who were struggling to forgive and were choosing to mask it with religiosity that before they could remove the speck of dust from the eye of another they needed to remove the plank from their own eye. Usually those who teach this passage conclude that Jesus' message is that we should not condemn another of sinning until we are pretty sure our lives are moving toward sinlessness. And I suppose that is right, insofar as it goes. But I think that teaching misses the real impact of what Jesus is saying.

"I don't think Jesus meant that we should have a vague awareness of our own capacity to sin and our need for forgiveness. I think that the plank symbolizes something deeper. Jesus meant that we have to understand that we could easily be guilty of the things we rush to condemn in others—the exact same things. I think he was saying that those things we are quickest to denounce in others are the things most likely to be present in ourselves. I get my ideas on this from him, Barry. They are not a product of the 'secular mind' you mentioned.

"The secular mind changes all of the time, and few people pay much heed. But words like Jesus' are different. They tend to get people killed, in more ways than one. They are just too hard to accept, so we have to get rid of them by banishing them from the village or burning them at the stake or refusing to associate with people who believe them and even sometimes nailing them to two pieces of wood shaped like a lowercase *t*.

"Barry, I'm going to throw out an odd phrase, one that will help you a great deal. It's sort of a mantra of mine. 'Resistance is your ally.' It's your ally, not your enemy, because it shows you that what you are doing is not working. Applied here, that means that Jim Grendell is not really your nemesis. In fact, he is likely to be the best teacher you have ever had, if you are willing to humble yourself and learn from him. The things you believe you see in him may well be in him. But that is less important than the fact that your reaction to them indicates beyond a reasonable doubt that they are firmly lodged in you."

Barry could not take anymore. He stood up and raised his voice to a level that surprised even him.

"Enough, Elliott!" he thundered. "That is so far out of line, and you are out of line. How dare you? I got crucified by the board tonight, led by Grendell. They called into question the essence of my existence as a man. I came to you for help sorting it out, and instead you suggest that the problem is me and you actually take Jim's side. You are no better than them!"

Barry snatched his coat and headed for the foyer. "Let me tell you this, Elliott. You may have a lot of wisdom. But you also have the capacity to kick a man when he is down. I am trying to courageously confront a self-righteous, manipulative bully who hides who he really is behind a veneer of piousness and emotion and who is about to divide my church, and instead you tell me that the problem is me. With friends like you ..." Barry let the thought die and instead opened the front door. "Thanks a lot, Elliott, for a lovely, condemning evening."

With that, Barry was out the door.

FIFTEEN MINUTES INTO HIS DRIVE, Barry pulled out his cell phone and called a gruff apology to Elliott. He told him that he knew Elliott was only trying to help, but his words had been ill-timed. Barry went on to say that he needed some space from Elliott, and he needed to tend to the problems in his church and home by himself for a while.

Elliott said that he understood but also offered to be available should Barry need him.

Elliott closed the phone call by saying, "You have put way more than your toe into the water, Barry. Tonight you got close to full-body immersion. You have the right and the ability to get out of the water should you choose. You don't have to go any farther. But I believe in my heart that you have the courage and fortitude to dive into the deep water and confront whatever it is that awaits you there."

Barry switched off his phone and sighed. "Right, deep water. Like I'm going to go there. I'm up to my neck as it is," Barry mumbled to himself as he continued the drive home. At the last moment, he swung his car toward the church, pulled into the parking lot, let himself in, and sat in his office, looking out the window.

The window framed Jim's warehouse across the street, gray and formless in the weak security lights. And Barry thought about how when it is dark outside and there is a light behind you, you can see what is outside the window and a reflection of yourself, both at the same time.

CHAPTER 5

The Deepest Water

You sound as if you are really hurting," said Henry. It was early morning after a sleepless night, and Barry had called his old friend, mostly to have someone to talk to who was not involved in his immediate situation.

"It feels like the lowest point of all," Barry replied. "Not only is the situation at the church terrible, but it feels like I have lost Elliott as well. Last night was really painful in every way imaginable."

"I can understand," said Henry. "I can't explain why Elliott does what Elliott does; I only know that he always has other people's good in mind. I guess he is like a surgeon in that way—he has to hurt you to heal you. Not that Elliott is your savior . . ."

"I know what you're saying," said Barry. "I know only God can save me in this situation, but I also know that I need to be involved in that process. I'm just not sure what to do next."

Barry tried to work on his upcoming sermon all morning, but he was tired, worried, and distracted. Part of him just wanted to escape, to take the day off and sit in a dark movie theater or find a solitary corner in the public library downtown where he could be alone with his thoughts and concerns.

Midmorning, Stephanie Perkins, the church's youth intern, had asked for a few minutes of Barry's time. He had agreed wearily. Stephanie often came to Barry to talk through issues and struggles she was facing, and she always seemed to be able to lift Barry's spirits through her praise of him. To hear Stephanie tell it, Barry was just short of Jesus in his empathy and skill with people. He knew well of Stephanie's insecurities and personal struggles, but there were times when her words were balm to his soul.

But the lift was always short-lived. After Stephanie had left his office, Barry stared at his laptop screen and realized that his ministry and sense of calling were a mess. A desultory lunch of a wilted fast-food salad at his desk alone did nothing to lift Barry's spirits, nor did the e-mail that arrived in his in-box as he was tossing the remains of his salad in the wastepaper basket.

The e-mail was from Jim, and despite its relatively conciliatory tone, it was a bombshell. Jim wrote that he had been unfair the previous night in saying that he was speaking for many members of the church without identifying who they were. He said that some people didn't want to be identified, but there were some who took their responsibilities as church leaders seriously and wanted to go on record. And then he named names. Five of the names were people who had been on the committee that had called Barry to First Community.

These people had been Barry's supporters and primary cheerleaders during his time at First Community. He knew that the changes he had been making had created some tension, but he had assumed that the support of these leaders, many of whom had been at the church for decades, was solid. Nothing he had heard led him to believe otherwise. Hearing now that this was not true devastated Barry.

Near the end of his rope, he called Sophia's cell-phone number. He got her voice mail, then remembered that she had gone to visit a friend of hers a couple of hours away.

Now at the end of his rope, he dialed Elliott Stevens.

Gracious as always, Elliott agreed to meet once again with Barry. Over the phone, as he spilled the story of his last twelve hours, Barry thought he noticed something different in Elliott's responses. He sounded softer, more empathic. And so Barry headed to Elliott's house.

The day was gray and chilly, a lot like Barry's heart. As he walked the circular driveway in front of Elliott's house and climbed the steps to the front door, Barry's legs felt heavy and stiff. He thought that he had never been more tired in his life.

Elliott opened the door, took Barry's coat, and seated him in the study. He excused himself and returned a few minutes later with a pot of hot tea and two mugs. Barry accepted the tea with gratitude and sank back into the couch.

"Barry, I am so sorry to see you hurting like this," Elliott began after he sat down. "How can I be of help?"

"Bottom line, Elliott, I'm out of answers and out of hope. This is worse than before. Up till now I have felt that my professional abilities were in question. Now it feels that I as a person, the very core of who I am, is inadequate. I really don't think I feel sorry for myself. But I do feel like a failure with very few options left."

Elliott was quiet for a long time, just looking into Barry's eyes. Barry took several sips of his tea and felt the warmth seep into his bones. Elliott's eyes seemed sad somehow. For the first time, it occurred to Barry that Elliott must have suffered some too in his life.

"Barry, I think most of all you need to rest today," Elliott finally said. "But there are a few things I would like to talk through with you, if you agree."

"Elliott, I'm at the point where I'm ready to try anything. I am at the end of my own resources."

Elliott smiled. "Barry, you have no idea how good it is to hear you say that. It means that you are diving into the deep water. It is important that you remember that things often have to get worse before they can get better, but I do think things are probably at about the lowest point they are going to get for you."

"I truly hope so," sighed Barry.

Elliott stood up and ran his hand through his white hair.

"Okay, Barry. I want to make only a couple of points today. Because I think that the best thing you can do today is to go home and get some sleep . . . don't even think about going back to the office. I will get right down to it.

"First, a question for you. How would you say that success in ministry is most often defined, especially in the professional circles you run in?"

"That's easy," replied Barry. "At its most elemental, pastors judge other pastors a success or failure based on three measures: attendance and membership, rate of church growth, and quality of church facilities. Most of us know that there are spiritual dynamics that transcend these things—some of the healthiest churches are the small to midsized ones. But at the end of the day, the 'winners' have rapidly growing churches and are either in a building program or have a new, modern facility.

"Another thing," Barry continued, "is that when people talk church growth these days, it is mostly of a certain kind, at least for suburban pastors like me. The true mark of success is reaching young families. Pastors who are seen to be successful always talk about how many kids are running around in their churches."

"That's pretty much what I thought," said Elliott. "Now, you know better than this. I am aware of that. But, all other things being equal, you would rather pastor a healthy church with significant growth and a nice new facility than a healthy church with a worn-down building and growth that has peaked at 250. Is that fair to say?"

"I don't like to say yes, but yes," answered Barry.

"That's okay," said Elliott with a chuckle. "It is a very human reaction. But the point remains that even if we know better, we often judge ourselves by the prevalent standards around us. That's hard enough. But in your case, Barry—and you are nowhere near alone in this—combine those expectations with elements of your personal story and the combination can be emotionally lethal."

"What part of my personal story?" asked Barry.

Elliott fiddled absentmindedly with the pens on his desk, then walked around the desk and sat down in his chair, facing Barry again.

"The part of your story in which you have received messages that you are not adequate as a man. That if people really knew you, they would see that you are a fraud, that you don't have what it takes in spite of how you might look on the outside. You have received that message at a number of points in your life, beginning in childhood, and I believe you have internalized it, as so many men do."

Elliott continued, "And when we internalize that message, it leads us into behaviors that are destructive to ourselves and those around us. Worst of all, it blinds us to the very things which could heal us.

"Barry, I want you to consider the possibility that Jim represents for you that core message—that you are not adequate, that you don't have what it takes, that if people knew the truth, they would know you are a fraud."

"I am willing to go with that, at least for a minute, Elliott," Barry said. "But what does it mean?"

"Great question, Barry. What it means is that instead of holding up your fears and insecurities to the light where they can be exposed and healed, you are transferring them over to Jim Grendell. Jim is outside of yourself, so you can take those anxieties and despise them in another person because it is safer than seeing them in yourself.

"But this creates an insurmountable problem because you don't get healed and you miss the real lesson Jim has for you."

"Elliott, you mentioned last time that Jim could be the best teacher I ever had. I Red Zoned over that idea, as you would say, but I am ready to hear what you meant."

"Barry, you are showing real courage now," Elliott replied. "You are in the crucible and you are ready to learn. I believe that as bad as things are right now, they are about to get better. Sometimes things have to get worse before they can get better, and you are the lowest you will go, I believe. I think you can take heart in that," Elliott said with a smile.

"Barry, remember one of the things we learned together, what I have referred to as a mantra of mine?"

"Yeah. Resistance is your ally," Barry answered.

"That's right," Elliott said. "And that is where Jim can be your teacher. Jim exposes in you the doubts and darkness you fear. He has done you a great favor by behaving in ways that have brought these things out in you. You have met real resistance in Jim. And this is good, because what resistance is best at is showing us that the strategies we are employing are not working."

Elliott stood up again and leaned against his desk. "When we meet resistance, we can go one of three ways, Barry. We can ignore it and push ourselves deeper in denial. We can wage war against it, as you have been doing. Or we can do what I believe you are about to do: we can pause and reflect on why what we are doing is not working and then change our approach."

"What exactly am I doing that is not working?" Barry asked.

"You are trying to compensate for your own self-doubt by papering it over with achievement. And you are missing the opportunity to care for people on a deep level because you have not been honest with yourself at the deepest level.

"Here's the thing, Barry. Jim is really not your problem. He is a symbol of the congregation as a whole, especially the older members. He is there to show you something very important. He is teaching you that the resistance you have felt at the church is not about selfishness or lack of willingness to change—they know they need change or they would not have hired you—but it is about their need to feel that they still matter, that they have a contribution to make in spite of the fact that they are smaller and less consequential than they used to be.

"As much as they want you to minister to others, Barry, you can't do it without them. And they are willing. But the truth is that they need ministry first."

Elliott paused to allow this to sink in. After a few seconds, Barry began to speak slowly. "But I am afraid that if I do that, they will just become more inwardly focused and then I won't ... we won't ..." Barry's voice trailed off.

"What are you afraid of, Barry?" Elliott asked with real tenderness.

"I'm afraid that if that happens, we won't grow and we will miss out on the chance to really have an impact on the community," Barry replied.

Still with consummate tenderness, Elliott said, "And, Barry, you are afraid that you will not be deemed a success, in your own eyes or in the eyes of others, aren't you?"

Barry's eyes began to sting and he lowered his head to hide the beginning of tears. "I'm afraid that I won't be good enough, that I won't do all that God wants me to do. I'm afraid that I will disappoint him and let him down."

"And so you fight that tooth and nail, fight Jim, fight resistance, fight with your last breath the fear that you won't measure up," Elliott said. "Barry, don't you think it is time to stop fighting and to start pastoring? Don't you think it's time to face up to your shadow side rather than fight it or ignore it? Don't you think God will meet you there and begin to heal you if you ask him? This is what Jim is teaching you, Barry. He is teaching you to be honest with God and yourself, to give up the ambitions that are a product of your own fears and instead to be ambitious for loving God and those in your life as well."

Elliott sat down in his chair and slumped in it. He seemed tired. The two men said nothing for many minutes.

Finally Elliott spoke. "Barry, are you completely spent or do you have a little more time?"

"I am totally spent, but I have more time. I know this is important," Barry answered.

"We have talked a lot about your projecting your shadow side onto Jim," Elliott began, "and how important it is to believe that he is actually your ally and teacher if you will pay attention to the fact that your strategy is not working. But it is also important that you know that other people will project things onto you as well and that the damage from that can be just as great as your own projection."

"I know that members of a congregation project onto their pastors," said Barry. "But I would love to hear your take as well."

"Barry, congregations tend to project two things onto their pastors: God, and their own fathers—or in the case of a female pastor, their mothers. When things are going well, the pastor can feel on top of the world. It is as if God has taken on tangible form for the congregation, and it is as if they now have the perfect father, regardless of how flawed their real fathers were."

Elliott leaned forward with an effort, but his eyes were alive again.

"This is the most dangerous time for a pastor. When you begin to believe the things adoring people are saying about you, you run the risk of deceiving yourself and them, and in many ways you are set up for a fall. It is a fact that many pastors carry feelings of inadequacy and a fear of failure within them. And those adoring words can feel like balm to a pastor's soul, especially since most people expect their pastor to care for them and never really stop to ask if the pastor is being cared for. This is the confusion people experience between role and self. Your role as pastor gathers the praise and the projected blame. Those words of praise and those biting criticisms aren't about you personally; they're directed at your role. The only way these words from the congregation can be about you is if you let them be about you.

"The pastor, missing the distinction between role and self, can begin to depend on this affirmation. For many it becomes an intoxicant, and they lose perspective, and they are set up for a world of hurt. I don't need to lay that out for you, do I, Barry?"

Barry shook his head. He had several friends who had suffered greatly by trying to salve their emotional pain in inappropriate ways.

"You have to realize that the adoring words are not really about you at all, even if the person saying them may be legitimately fond of you. All pastors have to realize that they are the repositories of the hopes, dreams, and aspirations of their followers. This becomes unhealthy when a person attaches to you because they believe you can provide for them a quality of relationship they have not experienced before. This is often because of unsatisfying adult relationships, but more often than not it goes back to childhood experiences in which the person was not cared for or loved well, perhaps by a parent who was preoccupied or was incapable of expressing intimate emotions."

Barry nodded. He was thinking of how his interactions with Stephanie, his adoring youth intern, often gave him a short-lived emotional lift.

Elliott seemed to read Barry's mind. "I think in your own case, there is a staff intern who plays this role in your life. Fortunately, you are wise enough to see this, I believe. You see intuitively that the more needy a person is, the more that person will project onto you the expectation of the perfect parent, the one who will heal you. Your example is the five people named in Jim's e-mail this morning. As hard as this is to say, Barry, the ones who express the most adoration of you are the most dangerous ones.

"It is not that they are bad people," Elliott emphasized, "or that they are out to do you harm. The danger comes when you start to believe that what they are seeing in you is actually you. Because when that adoration wears off and the pastor is revealed to be an imperfect person just like everyone else, the ones who adored the pastor before are often the ones to turn most viciously against him. And often this is too much for pastors to handle emotionally."

Elliott moved to his cherry cabinet, opened it, grabbed a marker from his desk, and wrote on the whiteboard:

Role versus Self

He then wrote:

When someone adores you, it is about their neediness, not about your spectacular qualities

"Barry, I know that you don't see adoration as your problem right now," said Elliott with an understanding smile. "But the adoration is the flip side of the anger you are now facing. They are not different things but rather part of the same unhealthy process."

Barry could not remember when he last felt energized. Now he felt more tired than ever. But he also felt something stirring in his soul, something fiery and hopeful.

"Elliott, I am bone tired and I need to go. But I think I understand. The struggles are really not about Jim at all, and I have let my distraction with that relationship obscure the fact that the problem is in me and that I can't address the problems of others until I see this for what it is."

Elliott nodded in agreement, not quite suppressing an enthusiastic smile.

Barry said, "I feel like I have crossed a bridge of some kind. Somehow I feel like I'm starting to see myself and the situation I find myself in with some clarity. It's not crystal clear yet, but it is coming into focus. I really do have to see that resistance is my ally and then live as if I actually believe it."

Elliott escorted Barry to the front door. "You used the metaphor of a bridge, Barry. As we say goodbye, I will use another metaphor. I believe that today you chose to dive into the deep water. It was the best of decisions, my friend."

CHAPTER 6

On the Right Track

For the first time in what seemed like forever, Barry and Sophia had a night together at home. After dinner, they sat together in the living room in front of a fire talking, trying to reconnect and reviewing the happenings of the last week.

"Barry, there's something I need to tell you, and I have a feeling you're not going to be happy," said Sophia, tentatively.

"Let me guess . . . Jake and school," Barry replied.

"I had a feeling you'd guess," sighed Sophia. "His teacher called again. She said his attitude is better but that his performance isn't improving noticeably. She's getting concerned now like we are, because unless this turns around soon, his grade in this class will be permanent and will affect his GPA for college applications.

"Look, I know you feel like I don't stay on Jake enough," Sophia continued, "but I am really trying to stay on top of this, to encourage him while at the same time letting him know the seriousness of the situation."

"I know you are, honey," Barry replied. "And I need to say again just how out of line I was in the kitchen the other day. I know you care about this every bit as much as I do. I guess that I just don't understand what is going on with Jake. We both know how smart he is. I just can't figure out what is keeping him from doing good work in this class."

Barry and Sophia stared into the fire for a while, listening to the flaming logs snap and pop.

"I wonder . . ." Barry began, and then trailed off. "I wonder if we have been looking at this the wrong way. We know Jake is smart; we know he has always worked hard in class before. I wonder if the problem is not Jake but is instead something else. Or some*one* else. I'm starting to think that the issue may not be Jake after all but that it's his teacher."

Barry warmed to his idea. "Yeah, I think that's it. We need to change the boy's teacher. Transfer him to another class. The more I think about it, the more sure I am that it's the solution."

The mudroom door banged open and in a few moments Jake walked into the room.

"Hey, Mom, Dad," the teenager said as he headed upstairs to his room.

"Just a sec, bud," said Barry. "I want to run something by you."

Jake kissed his mom playfully and sat down at the fireplace, soaking up its heat. "Sure. What's up, Dad?"

"Your mom and I have been talking about this class deal," Barry began. Jake's eyes shifted nervously to Sophia, who raised her eyebrows as if to say "hear your dad out."

"Jake," Barry continued, "I wonder if you think that maybe a change of teacher in the form of a class transfer would be a good idea. We all know that you've got to do well in all of your classes from here on out to get into the kind of school we all hope you can go to, and I think it's important to catch this thing right now before it gets too late in the semester.

"I don't think you are slacking, really, Jake. But I do know we need to act, and act now, and if the teacher is the issue, we need to make a move to get you out of there. What do you think?"

Jake ran his hand through his dark, bushy hair and played with his yellow Lance Armstrong bracelet for a moment. "Gee, Dad. I don't know. I don't know if that's really the problem, or ... I mean I like my teacher and everything, but you know ... I mean, if you think that's the right thing to do, Dad, that's cool. I'll go along with whatever you say."

Jake got up, kissed his mom's forehead again, and bounded up the stairs to his room.

"Great!" exclaimed Barry. "That's it. Soph, I'll get on this first thing in the morning, make some calls and work it out. I know this is the right move!"

BARRY USUALLY WENT FOR A three-mile run each morning before going to work. Today it was brisk and bright as he pounded the pavement of the streets in his neighborhood. Barry often did some of his best thinking and planning while running, and this morning he was organizing his thoughts for how to respond to the most recent board meeting.

Convinced now that he had moved too fast in implementing changes without taking to heart the feelings of the core members in the congregation, Barry decided to make amends by starting with the most visible part of the church's life—the worship service.

After Barry finished his run with a hard sprint, he finalized his thinking. He planned to head in to the office and break the worship service down element by element, decide what he could change without compromising his commitment to reaching new people, and make the changes. Most important, he would make sure that he got buy-in from key leaders first.

After a shower and a bagel, Barry headed for his office. He said hi to his administrative assistant, briefly checked his e-mail, and then pulled out the folder in which he kept ideas for worship services as well as a written evaluation of the service, which he completed each week.

He poured a cup of coffee, took out a legal pad and a gel pen, and began to make notes. Two hours later, he had developed the outline of a plan. He pushed back from his desk, stretched, checked his e-mail again, and then smacked his palm across his forehead. "Oh, man . . . I forgot!"

Barry picked up the phone and dialed Jake's school. He got the principal's voice mail and left a brief message saying that he would like to discuss Jake's classroom situation and perhaps make a class transfer.

Barry hung up the phone and sat still for a moment. Slowly, a smile spread across his face. He felt good for the first time in a long time. Rather than reacting to events, Barry felt like he was being proactive, moving forward and tackling tough issues, making change happen instead of being the victim of unanticipated events.

After lunch, Barry worked the phones for a while, setting up meetings—two for that afternoon—with core members of the board. He wanted to move on discussing his plans for changing the worship service while he was still on a roll.

Barry tackled administrative tasks for a while and spent a bit of time troubleshooting several problems with his staff, and at 3:30 he headed out for a coffee meeting with Kim James, a board member who had a particular interest in the church's worship ministry.

Kim sipped on a tall decaf while Barry gulped a double latte and laid out his ideas.

In essence, Barry wanted to have a blended service, merging elements of both the traditional and the contemporary. He was willing to add two hymns to each service, to resume the highly personal "prayers for the church," which he had removed because it felt too "insiderish" to attract newcomers, and to use video clips only sparingly. In addition, Barry was willing to vary his sermon planning, adding some straight Bible exposition to his topical sermons designed to attract young families.

Barry felt that he was giving up an awful lot, and delaying his dream of leading a church thoroughly structured to attract nonchurchgoing young families, but he reasoned that Elliott was right that he had to go slower and care for the older members.

He finished his presentation and then asked for Kim's comments. She seemed open to Barry's ideas but also a little less enthused than Barry had hoped. It wasn't that she was resistant—in fact, she complemented Barry on his willingness to bring the changes up rather than simply making them—but her support seemed just a little guarded.

His 4:30 meeting with another board member went much the same way, with a polite reception and a modest expression of support. Barry was a little curious but was way too excited to be discouraged. After the meetings, Barry returned to his office and adjusted his plan to take into account some of the feedback he had received. The next board meeting was in two nights, and Barry wanted to be sure that he had done his homework and gotten adequate feedback prior to presenting his ideas to the gathered church leaders.

Barry was fully engaged in the change process for the next two days, meeting with as many board members as he could, briefing the church staff and seeking their input, and working to touch base pastorally with several of the older members.

On the home front, Jake's principal had returned his call and agreed to meet with Barry and Sophia early the next week to discuss Jake's problems in class and the potential of moving him to another class.

The night before the board meeting, Barry and Sophia again lounged before the fire. Barry was watching North Carolina and Duke battle it out in college basketball while Sophia read a book. When the Tar Heels had the game well in hand, he muted the TV and turned to his wife.

"You know, I'm feeling pretty good about things, Soph," Barry began.

Sophia lowered her book and smiled at Barry. "I'm really glad to hear that, baby. Why are you feeling so good?"

"I think there is some real momentum here," Barry replied. "I think the board is going to be really responsive to the worship service changes, and I also think I'm going to get a lot of support for being willing to subordinate my own desires for the greater good. Now, of course, the changes will come, but I think this is going to give me some political capital for when the really transformational decisions come.

"Also," Barry continued, "I like that we are on top of the situation with Jake instead of reacting to it. I like that we have talked with him and that you and I are in this together instead of pitted against one another.

"And again," Barry continued, "I know that conflict between us was my fault because I was somehow connecting Jake to my own desires for achievement. I really owe Elliott a huge favor for helping me see that and helping me see that I need to bring the church along more slowly."

Sophia smiled again. "Things do seem to be going well, Barry. And I respect so much the strides you are making. But I also don't want you to get your hopes up too high."

"What do you mean?" Barry frowned.

"Nothing really negative, Barry. I don't want to dampen your enthusiasm, which makes me really glad to see. But the conflict at the church won't be solved overnight, and so I don't want you to be crushed when things move slower than you might want. And I still have a feeling that we haven't dug quite deep enough into Jake's struggles at school. Call it a hunch ... or a mother's intuition."

THE MEMBERS OF THE CHURCH BOARD settled into their seats, and Barry opened with prayer. Jim Grendell led the group through a number of routine matters. As Barry glanced around the room, he sensed that there was much less tension than the last meeting, but there was still a tentative reserve in the air.

Barry had requested time to speak about his ideas for the worship service changes, and when the group came to that point in the agenda, Jim turned the meeting over to Barry.

Barry cleared his throat and began to speak. "As I'm sure all of you know, our last meeting was a very difficult one for me. I was caught off guard by some of the concerns Jim expressed and that a number of you shared. That was a tough blow, and I still wish that those concerns had been communicated differently, but that is past now. As it turns out, I agree with some of the concerns.

"I am a person who is drawn by vision and gets wholeheartedly committed to making a vision happen. When I came here to be your pastor, I had a clear mandate to transform the church into a worshiping community which would reach young families who were not connected to another church. I have tried to do that. But at the same time, I have failed in some of my duties to pastor this congregation.

"At times, I have moved too fast and taken too little care for the faithful, older members of this church. I have been so focused on reaching new members that I have sometimes neglected to show enough care and concern for the opinions of those who sacrificed and built this church. I am very sorry for that.

"I intend to be a better pastor and to go at a slower pace, and I would like to demonstrate that by suggesting some changes to the worship service."

Barry passed out a memo and walked the board through his proposed changes, taking care to mention that he had incorporated a number of changes after his meetings with individual board members.

The members of the board asked a few clarifying questions, and Barry asked them to review and think about the memo and to have feedback for him at the following week's meeting. The meeting ended with nothing eventful happening, and Barry breathed a sigh of relief as he closed the gathering with prayer.

A few minutes later, Barry was in his office gathering his briefcase and coat for the ride home. There was a knock on the door, and three of the members of the board asked if they could come in for a brief chat.

Kim James spoke for the trio.

"Pastor, I think most of us appreciated your words tonight. I for one think you are very genuine. Others do as well. But I need to tell you there is some disappointment among some members."

Barry leaned back in his chair and exhaled deeply. "Okay, Kim, I am all ears."

"I don't know that I have much more to say, Barry, only—"

Bill, another member of the board, jumped in. "Barry, here's the deal. Some folks—some of the older folks you owned up to disregarding a bit—feel that you're throwing them some cosmetic changes in the worship service as a bone."

Bill paused, apparently expecting Barry to react, but Barry only nodded and said, "Go ahead, Bill."

Bill gathered his thoughts and continued. "I think there's a sense that 'if you give this guy an inch, he'll take a mile.' I think some people wonder if you're just making a strategic retreat here but you fully intend to keep moving your agenda forward anyway. I'm not saying that's the case, but there was a little talk of that. We're just saying that you need to pay attention to those perceptions."

Barry thanked them as they left the office. He lingered for a moment, letting his gaze fall again on the warehouse across the street. He was a little disheartened, to be sure, but surprised himself by not feeling devastated. As he snapped off his desk lamp, locked the office door, and headed for the parking lot, one thought was running through his brain: *Remember, Barry, resistance is your ally.*

CHAPTER 7
Thaw in Chicago

"I'm sorry I'm late," Barry gasped as he rushed into the principal's office. He fell into a chair next to Sophia and looked at the principal apologetically.

Richard Davis chuckled. "It's okay, Barry. I think our jobs have a lot in common, and I know that unexpected things often come up. Coffee?"

Barry declined and made himself comfortable in his chair. Both Barry and Sophia very much liked Principal Davis, a large, genial man with a booming laugh and an evident concern for kids.

"Sophia was telling me that things are busy at the church these days," said the principal. "I hope you are taking care of yourself."

"Doing the best I can," Barry replied. "But I cannot imagine that my schedule is busier than yours, Richard."

"Oh, I imagine about the same. But you are doing the Lord's work, Barry," said Richard with a laugh that filled the room.

"Richard, you know our point of view on that," said Sophia. "You are doing the Lord's work every bit as much as Barry. Except you have to chase hundreds of kids around all day!"

"Ah, Sophia, here's the part you don't get—chasing kids around all day keeps my figure trim and svelte." The principal patted his ample belly and let out a laugh that filled not only the room but the hallway outside as well.

Richard took a deep swallow of coffee from an enormous earthenware mug and focused on his visitors. "Okay, guys, what is this about Jake and his troubles in class?"

A little to Barry's surprise, Sophia took the lead in telling the story, detailing Jake's struggles, their conversations with his teacher, and the continued lack of progress Jake had demonstrated.

Richard listened attentively. When Sophia had finished, he got right to the point. "So you both feel that a change in class would be beneficial for Jake?"

"I'm pretty convinced of that," said Barry. "I think Sophia is a little less convinced than I am, but we both agree that something needs to change and change quickly. Jake has never had trouble of any kind in class before, and the only new dynamic I can think of in this situation is his teacher.

"I'm not saying the teacher is incompetent," Barry added quickly. "Just that there doesn't seem to be a spark and a connection that is going to help Jake learn and excel in the class. And you know better than anyone, Richard, how colleges start focusing on GPA from here on out."

"I do know that, Barry," Richard replied. The principal stroked his salt-and-pepper goatee for a moment.

"Barry, Sophia . . . you know that Jake and I have a good relationship, don't you?" asked Richard.

Both nodded their heads. "Jake really likes and trusts you, and so do we," Sophia agreed.

"I really love the kid too," said Richard. "And I want you to know that he really confides in me."

Barry and Sophia sat silently, listening.

"Now, we can orchestrate a class transfer for Jake, if that is what you all agree to," said the principal. "And that might work. It might possibly work . . ." Richard let his words trail out.

"You are hesitant for some reason, though," said Sophia.

"Yes, Sophia, I am hesitant. Let me say it again, we can do the transfer if need be. And I know both of you feel that time is of the essence, and I understand that, but I am going to suggest that you wait several days to make a final decision."

"Why the wait?" asked Barry, a little impatiently.

"Because there is something that I am going to tell you that I would like for you to take a couple of days to think about," answered Richard.

"Jake and I talk a lot as student and principal, and also I think he is someone who looks up to me a bit. I think I have some insight into the kid. I wonder, Barry, if you know how important your approval of him is to Jake." Richard looked up, directly into Barry's eyes.

The principal continued. "Yes, your approval is quite important to Jake. He wants you to respect and appreciate him. I believe he is absolutely sure that you love him." Richard gestured with his hand to bring Sophia into the conversation. "You both have done an extraordinarily good job of communicating love to Jake and that is absolutely foundational.

"But, guys, I'm not just talking about love. Barry, Jake very much wants your approval. I cannot speak for the young man, but I suspect that as he gets farther along in his high school career and realizes how important it is that he gets good grades for college applications, he feels more pressure than before to please you. Barry, you got good grades, you were gifted in sports, you have been successful professionally. Jake wants to live up to that. And that creates quite a lot of pressure for a kid."

Even though he didn't want to, Barry felt a little defensive inside. "Richard, I know that every kid wants to please their parents and that boys especially want to please their dad, but look, we have gone to great lengths to make sure that our kids know that we love them for who they are, not for what they do."

Barry glanced over at Sophia for support, but, curiously, her eyes were riveted on Richard.

"What Barry said is true," Sophia said. "But Richard, there is something we are missing, isn't there?"

"I think there might be, Sophia. I think there just might be," the principal said with a slight nod.

He turned his eyes to Barry. "Barry, the kid knows you love him. But that is not what I'm talking about here. I am not sure if Jake feels that you approve of him, that you affirm him. And there is quite a large difference between love on the one hand and affirmation and approval on the other."

Barry had experienced more emotion in the last several months than he could remember experiencing in his whole life, nearly, but Richard's words still hit him with devastating force. He felt a weight on his heart, but it wasn't defensiveness. Instead of answering right away, he felt intuitively that he should simply let the weight be there for the time being.

"I . . . I'm not sure how to respond to that," Barry said finally.

"And I don't know that you need to," the principal said quickly. "That's why I want you to let it sit for a few days. The connection I see, and that you have to decide if you see as well, is between Jake's desire to have your approval and affirmation and the fact that your anxiety level about Jake's future is rising as the time nears when he will go to college and leave your home. I believe he feels pressure because of this, and as we both know from athletic competition, the more pressure a person feels, the more likely they are to screw up."

Barry felt guilty, stunned, sad. But something was different this time. He also felt somewhere deep down inside his stomach a stirring. It also felt like nerves, but it felt more alive than that. It was a sort of enlargening of his heart, the sense that something good and alive was happening in his spirit. He felt crushed, but also strangely hopeful. He had no idea what to say.

Richard saved Barry from having to say anything. He drained his coffee mug and stood up. "Okay, guys, duty calls . . . I gotta run. Barry, don't you have a parishioner in need of a visit, or a sermon to write?" The principal let loose with another booming laugh.

"Yes. Thank you, Richard," Barry replied. "Thank you very much."

Almost before she knew what she was doing, Sophia reached out and grabbed the principal's hand. "Richard, you have no idea how much you may have helped. I am so grateful."

The principal appeared to be moved, and he reached out his two enormous hands, placing his left hand on Barry's shoulder and his right hand on Sophia's. "The two of you are good parents. And good friends. I wish all my kids had parents like you. You have a special kid. Just think about what I said, okay?"

As they made their way to their cars, Sophia slipped her hand into Barry's. "Honey, what do you think, how do you feel?"

"I'm not exactly sure," Barry answered. "Confused and hopeful at the same time. Does that make any sense?"

Sophia laughed, softly and joyfully, and said, "Yes, you have no idea how much sense it makes." She dropped her husband's hand. "Do you have time for lunch?"

Barry shook his head. "I have an appointment with Elliott."

Sophia smiled. "Okay. Hope it goes well."

Barry gave her a smile in return. "I'll see you later," he said as he squeezed his wife's shoulder and kissed the top of her head tenderly.

ELLIOTT OPENED HIS FRONT DOOR before Barry's hand had even reached the lion-head knocker. Elliott was wearing an old brown barn coat, faded blue jeans, and a broad smile.

"I have an idea," he said. "The spring thaw is starting to come, and it is warmer today than it has been in a while. Why don't we walk around my garden in the back while we chat?"

Barry said he was delighted with the idea, and the two men made their way to the rear yard of Elliott's large home.

Elliott's garden was enclosed neatly within a beautiful brick perimeter. Much of the garden lay fallow for the winter, but daffodils were visible.

"I love the daffodils," Elliott murmured, gesturing at the flowers. "They are beautiful and tough at the same time. Did you know that they actually poke through the snow? Some people call them soldiers because that is what they look like as they struggle to emerge."

They walked in silence around the perimeter of the garden. Like the man himself, Barry thought, Elliott's garden was ordered and elegant and managed to be approachable at the same time.

Elliott paused for a moment and stretched, letting out a huge pleasured yawn. "I love this weather," he beamed. "I love the crispness of it and the fact that you can breathe without damaging your lungs with frostbite, which is not a given in these Chicago winters. Actually, each season has its charms and beauties and reminders and hints of God."

He turned and touched Barry's arm lightly. "But enough about an older man's simple pleasures," he laughed. "Let's talk about you and what has happened in the last few days." With that, he led Barry to a simple stone bench and they sat down.

Elliott was silent, and so Barry began to tell his story of the last board meeting and his and Sophia's meeting with Richard Davis.

After he had finished the story, Barry said, "Elliott, things are becoming very clear for me on both the work and the home fronts about how to see resistance as my ally and how to lead change—first in my own life and then in the lives of others. But there are still a few missing pieces for me."

"What kind of missing pieces?" asked Elliott.

"I think that what I'm missing is the application. I feel like I have a much deeper understanding of myself and the dynamics of relationships, but I'm still not quite sure what to do with all of that."

"Barry, let's take these situations one at a time," Elliott replied. "First your home and then the church. If you can lead well in your home, then you can do so anywhere. In many ways, changing the way you relate to those you love the most is the hardest change of all.

"I want us to pause on one thing first, though," Elliott continued. "There is a little more that I want you to see from your conversation with Principal Davis, who, by the way, is an old friend of mine."

Why does that not surprise me? Barry thought with a smile he kept to himself.

Elliott kept talking. "Richard did an excellent job of drawing a distinction between love on the one hand and affirmation and approval on the other. It is possible, in a limited way, for a person to know that they are loved but to know also that they are not approved of or believed in deeply. And I also respect the fact that you did not respond defensively to Principal Davis's point. Because, my friend, a few short months ago, you would have exploded."

"You've got that right," Barry said with a wry smile.

"I want to go one step beyond just diagnosing the difference between love and affirmation in the ways that you relate to Jake," said Elliott. "I would like for you to consider *why* you might communicate love without affirmation to Jake. Do you have any ideas, Barry?"

Barry nodded. "I have wondered why myself. It seems to me that lack of communication about affirmation and approval might be something of a male syndrome, and so I could be following the male code of being reluctant to express feelings. But to be honest, usually I'm pretty open about those things. So I don't think that's the whole story."

Elliott nodded encouragingly, but Barry found himself at a loss for words.

After a minute, Elliott smiled. "Barry, I am going to risk sounding like a movie parody of a psychologist here, but I'll say this anyway: tell me about your relationship with your father."

"I thought you might mention that," Barry replied. "But he did a better job than I am doing, I'm afraid. He was gruff and tough like most men of his generation, but there was never a doubt that he loved us. He had very high expectations, but he was also reasonable. He was at all of my games that I can remember, and he made major school events, in spite of the fact that his business kept him very busy. He was a great dad. Demanding as all get out, but great."

"He sounds like a wonderful man," smiled Elliott. "Let me ask you this, Barry. How did you know when you had met his demands?"

"Hmm. I've never thought of it that way before." Barry frowned as he thought. "I guess I would have to say that I felt a lessening of the feeling of expectations coming from him. He never really said anything, but I could tell he was pleased."

"How exactly could you tell your dad was pleased with you?" pressed Elliott.

"I think it was just that . . . that he seemed to be less demanding. Just a moment . . . it just hit me that 'demanding' is a bit harsh. I would describe what I experienced from Dad as expectations more than demands."

"It is interesting that you chose the word 'demands,' though, Barry. Why do you think that was the word that first came to your mind?"

"That's another good question. Let me see . . . All right, maybe this is it. I think my dad had expectations of us but that I may have experienced those internally as demands. Maybe it was me who was doing the demanding of myself, because I wanted to please him so much."

Elliott was silent, but the gentle look in his eyes caused Barry to catch his breath.

"Oh, man," Barry breathed. "That's it. That's what Jake is experiencing from me. He knows I love him, but he doesn't know that he has done well enough for my demands to be lessened. I remember now . . . I never knew exactly what my dad was thinking. I assumed that he was pleased because the feelings of demand decreased when I did something I knew he liked, but I was never really quite sure if he . . ."

"If he what, Barry?" Elliott asked softly.

"If he really approved of me or not," said Barry. He puffed his cheeks, let an enormous breath out, and was quiet.

Barry looked stricken, so Elliott placed his hand on the younger man's shoulder kindly. "I know you have to leave for an appointment, so why don't we walk back to your car?"

Elliott kept his hand on Barry's shoulder as they walked back toward the front of the house.

As they stood by Barry's car, Elliott said, "Barry, if I may before you go . . . I don't want to sound trite here, but I think it would be helpful for you to think of Jake as a 'little Barry.' What you are providing Jake is precisely what your father, a good and loving man, provided you. The transforming change for you now, really the opportunity of a lifetime, is that you get the chance to provide Jake what you did not get as a young man. Can you begin to see this?"

Barry was afraid that his voice might crack if he spoke, so he nodded, squeezed Elliott's arm, and got into his car. Elliott watched as he drove away. It struck Barry that this man cared deeply for him.

As he drove back to his office, Barry turned off his cell phone so that he would have the chance to think and reflect. When he pulled into the parking lot and flipped the phone back on, he had a voice mail from Elliott.

"Barry, we have talked about the home front, and now you can go love your son the way you truly want to, by affirming and approving of him at the deepest level. Dive deeply into these waters this week. And if you have the time, will you please come see me next week? Then we can talk about how your new way of living can spill over into your pastoral leadership as well. Know that my thoughts, prayers, and deepest respect are with you, my friend."

THAT EVENING, BARRY WAS SITTING in the family room reading a book when Jake came in. Heading up the stairs, Jake paused and came back down when he saw his dad. He pulled his headphones off of his ears, slipped a CD from his portable player, and handed it to his father.

"Dad, this is the new U2 CD. You've probably never heard of them, have you?" Jake asked.

Barry chuckled inwardly at the patent assumptions of youth. U2's first album had been released while Barry was in high school, and in the years since then, the masterful Irish rock band's work had formed a sort of soundtrack for Barry's life, as it had for many others of his generation. Their passionate songs were about idealism, love, peace, justice, and mercy, the limitations and traps of the human heart, and the involvement of God, sometimes seemingly obscure, in the affairs of mankind. Along the way, they had become the most popular rock band in the world. Barry was amazed that he had never told his son of his love for the band.

"Yeah, Jake, I've heard of them," Barry said with a straight face.

"Cool," the son replied. "Anyway, the lead singer's dad died while he was writing songs for this CD, and two of the songs are about that. He wrote one the night his dad died, and the other one he performed at his dad's funeral.

"Anyway, it seems like they had kind of a rough relationship, even though it was close, and that Bono had to say some things in a song after his dad died that maybe he didn't get to say in person. And I was thinking I hope that never happens to us, Dad. Okay, anyway, that's it, that's all. Just thought you might like to take a listen. If you want to."

Jake bounded up the stairs but turned around sharply when he reached the top step. With a wide grin on his face, he blurted, "But you gotta get it back to me by tomorrow morning, Dad, and if you don't I might just have to take you out!"

Jake's shaggy head disappeared and Barry was left to contemplate the wonder of his boy, all at once vulnerable and nonchalant, wise and inexperienced in the ways of the world. Perhaps inexperienced to his benefit, Barry thought.

Barry rose from his recliner and put the CD in the stereo, settled back in his chair, and picked up the liner notes so that he could read the lyrics as he listened.

One of the songs Jake had mentioned, "Sometimes You Can't Make It on Your Own," reflected beautifully the timeless tensions between fathers and sons who love each other deeply but can't always figure out exactly how to express that love, often covering it up with conversation about "things."

The song acknowledged that sometimes fathers and sons play the role of adversary to one another, the son desperately wanting to be like or to understand his father even as he seeks to form his own identity separate from the man. And all the while, the father desires to bless the son he loves so much he could burst but struggles to separate his own fears and failures from his relationship with his child.

Needing to go to sleep, but not wanting to let the CD's spell dissipate, Barry forwarded the disc to its last song, which had an intriguing title: "Yahweh." The song was a prayer, nothing less than a psalm, really, and as Barry listened, he made the psalm his own prayer.

Take these hands
Teach them what to carry
Take these hands
Don't make a fist
Take this mouth
So quick to criticize
Take this mouth
Give it a kiss

As he listened and prayed, Barry's heart broke—for the love of his son and of his calling as a pastor, for his failures in both arenas, for the hope at the very center of the universe, for that which is already and that which is not yet.

CHAPTER 8

Back at Work

Barry and Elliott had agreed to meet in a restaurant for lunch the following week. Over grilled-chicken sandwiches, salads, fruit, and Diet Cokes, the two men caught up on the events of the last week.

Barry told his friend about his conversation with Jake and his moments listening to the U2 CD. Since that night, Barry's heart had been full and his mind active as he tried to orient his relationship with Jake around affirmation. He had prayed and spent a lot of time journaling, listening, thinking, and looking for ways in which he had communicated demands rather than approval. He and Jake had had several good talks. Talking about "deep" issues was a little awkward for both father and son, but they were each engaged and Barry had much hope for the days ahead.

Elliott listened, nodded approvingly, asked a lot of questions, and made a few suggestions. When the server brought coffee, he pushed his chair back from the table and smiled. "Okay, Barry. You have plunged into the deep water regarding your childhood and adolescence and your own parenting. You have emerged from the water in many ways a new man and a new father. I believe that you are well on your way to becoming a truly outstanding father. The road ahead will not always be easy—adolescence is always a trying time and there will be times when you will default back to your old pattern of being too demanding—but I am convinced that the road will be a good one.

"I am proud of you, if it is not too presumptuous of me to say such a thing. You have proven to be a man of heart and courage, one who is decisive but who is also tender. You are a good man, Barry Wolf," Elliott said with a twinkle in his eye.

"And now it is time for you to emerge from the deep water concerning your life and your calling as a pastor. Are you ready for that?"

Barry leaned forward and spoke firmly. "Yes. I am ready."

"Wonderful, Barry," Elliott replied. "Now, may we talk about what this might look like?"

"Absolutely," Barry answered. "I have called a special board meeting tomorrow night, and the timing is perfect to set the stage for what is to come."

"Right," said Elliott. "I'd like to ask you several questions now." Barry nodded for Elliott to go ahead.

"First," Elliott began, "summarize what you believe to be the core challenges facing the church at the present time."

Barry had done a lot of thinking about this and was ready with his answer. "I think three things. The first thing is the issue of pastoral leadership, how they want their pastor to lead versus what I believe effective pastoral leadership to be. A chaplain versus a change leader is one way of looking at it.

"The next thing is mission—what the church is supposed to be about, what our purpose is. Are we about caring for those who are there, or are we about reaching young families not connected with the church? Can we balance those two things?

"The last issue is the worship service. This is kind of a subcategory of the second issue of mission, but in any church, the worship service sparks controversy and strong feelings because it is the central shared experience of the church. The question as I see it is, Can we make the worship service relevant to the people we are trying to reach without alienating older members of the church?"

Elliott nodded. "So you see the three challenges as pastoral leadership, mission, and the worship service."

Barry nodded.

"Fair enough," Elliott said. "Now, if you would, tell me how you plan to address each of these challenges with the board."

Barry had been thinking a lot about this too, and he didn't hesitate to answer. "I have to admit my failings first. I have to say that I moved too fast without taking the feelings of many of the members of the congregation into account. I didn't listen well enough. Then I have to be firm in charting a course, a mission for us. But instead of charging ahead, I have to involve them at every step of the process, even going slower in making changes than I would like, if that becomes necessary to bring everyone along." Barry paused. "Am I on track so far, Elliott?" Elliott thought for a moment. "Well, yes, you are on track. But I have another question for you. Why is it that you see yourself as the center of solving the church's challenges?" Barry was puzzled. "I'm not sure I understand what you mean."

"I mean that as you were moving through your solutions for the three challenges, you saw yourself as the primary actor in solving the problems. No doubt, you talked a lot about involving others, but you were still the main one involved. But the work is not yours. The work belongs to the congregation."

"But someone has to lead them!" Barry exclaimed. "I know that I have to be less forceful and more of a guide than a dictator, but leading is still my job."

"You are exactly right, Barry. The question is not who the leader is but rather the nature of the leadership you exercise." Elliott clasped his hands together. "Remember our conversation about the difference between technical and adaptive change?"

"Sure," Barry answered. "Technical change is change on the surface, using strategies and knowledge familiar to us. Sometimes technical change is good and even necessary, but it is not deep change. Adaptive change is deep change on the level of values, beliefs, and behavior."

"You've got it, Barry. Here's my point. The change that your church needs to experience is not technical change but adaptive change. And that means you must be an adaptive leader. And that first means, counterintuitively, that they must do the work, not you. Your job is simply to prepare the ground for change, ask the right questions, and keep the group focused."

Barry started to speak but caught himself. He gathered his thoughts. "What you are saying is that my solutions were temporary fixes. I see what you're saying, but I know I have to start somewhere, and that is the hard thing for me. Exactly where do I start?"

Elliott nodded, looking deeply satisfied. "Ah, yes . . . the question! Fortunately, an answer is at hand. In fact, you have the answer, Barry. Think."

Barry thought. "Adaptive change requires change at the level of values and beliefs, which results in changes in behavior. So whatever I do has to involve leading them to consider what their values and beliefs actually are. And they have to answer that question for themselves and to decide how and if they want to change."

Elliott was beaming. "Exactly, Barry. Keep going."

"That means that my role is to be the guy setting the context for change, keeping the key issues before the group, making sure that they stay focused on the real questions and don't default to technical discussions. And if I allow the issue to be my leadership, my ministry philosophy, my role as pastor, that allows the board to escape the real questions, which involve a deeper understanding of their own values and beliefs."

Elliott nodded vigorously. "And there is no question that there is tension and disagreement within the leadership at the church. There is the strong oppositional front man, Jim; there are others who follow Jim's lead; others who are more on 'your' side. But you see, if they continue to see this thing as divided between sides, they can never move forward. In truth, you are really not the issue. The issue is conflict on the level of values and beliefs within the community of the church. And your job is to shift the work to them.

"You see," Elliott continued, "everyone in the church has needs that you as the pastor cannot satisfy. Everyone is looking to you to heal them. If you try to do this, you will burn yourself out or exhaust your emotional and spiritual resources and be set up for a very big fall. You can never meet the expectations set for you. Fortunately, you don't have to."

"Because," Barry said, "all I really have to do is show them that the answers lie within the community itself, and then I have to keep them from making the issue about me or some other technical matter. Do you know how many pastors don't know this, Elliott? Do you know how many friends I have who spend their careers trying to meet the expectations set for them by their congregations, and the ones they have of themselves? And nothing ever really changes, in spite of all the effort, energy, pain, and heartbreak."

Elliott's face became sad. "Yes, I know. This is the great tragedy of professional ministry in this time and culture. All of this effort trying to master lists of principles of leadership or to ingest church growth methods or to add a service or take away a service or start a ministry to reach young people ... all this change, all this activity without a pause to consider the church's fundamental beliefs about itself, what is important to it and its role. And good men and women who are pastors are destroyed by their churches, or they destroy themselves in a variety of heartbreaking ways."

Barry felt a deep sadness as well, but one laced with hope. "And many other pastors and their congregations arrive at an unspoken bargain, in which the status quo becomes king and they quietly go about their lives together, never even coming close to their redemptive potential in their communities. But Elliott, I am becoming very convinced that it does not have to be that way." Barry set his jaw. "And it's not gonna be that way at First Community."

Elliott was smiling again. "Good, Barry. I love to see the fight in you, love even more to see your energies channeled in the right direction. Now about that meeting tomorrow night—"

"Yes, that meeting," Barry interrupted. "Elliott, can you help me set an agenda, to clarify the questions I need to ask to get them focused on adaptive change?"

"No," Elliott replied.

"No?" Barry was startled.

"No," Elliott said again. "Because you do not need for me to do that. You have what you need inside of yourself to figure this out and lead it. You know more than I do, and you can do a much better job of setting an agenda than I could."

Elliott signed the credit-card slip for lunch and stood up to put on his coat. "Barry, I have more faith in you than you realize. I have been able to help you along the way, I hope. But all I have done with you is to prepare you to do the same thing with your congregation. It's all about understanding that resistance is your ally. It is all about choosing to live in the Blue Zone rather than the Red Zone. And it is all about leading adaptive change. You can do it, Barry. You *will* do it."

With a smile and a wink but without another word, Elliott left the restaurant.

THAT AFTERNOON, BARRY WALKED OVER to Jim Grendell's warehouse. He caught Jim by surprise, but the warehouse owner recovered quickly and pulled up a gray folding chair for Barry.

"Jim, this is really unusual for me to ask, but I need to lead the meeting tomorrow night," Barry began.

Jim was visibly irritated. "Now, Pastor, you know that a big issue now is people feeling like you are controlling, and if you go and do things like demand to run meetings, that impression is only going to deepen. Now, I will run the meeting and make sure there is plenty of time for you to talk about the things you need to talk about."

Barry leaned forward in his chair and smiled. "Jim, I very much respect and appreciate your role as the board's chairperson. I am not trying to grab control. I'm asking you for the privilege of leading the main discussion. I assure you that I have no intention of controlling the meeting, and you will always have the prerogative as chairperson to rein me in. I would really appreciate your help on this. This is really important for all of us."

Jim shifted in his chair and grumbled a bit but eventually relented. Barry left the gloom of the aging warehouse and walked back across the street to his office. He poked his head in the door of each staff member's office to say hi and check in. Then he went into his office and shut the door, took out his ever-present white legal pad, and set to work planning for his first meeting as an adaptive leader.

That night, Barry had a long talk with Sophia, and he and Jake played a few spirited games of table tennis. Barry woke up the next morning well rested and full of energy. As the day went on, Barry fine-tuned his sermon for Sunday, attended to some administrative matters, took a quick swing by the hospital to visit a church member healing from surgery, and made a final draft of his agenda for the meeting.

As the time for the meeting approached, Barry lingered near the door to the conference room and greeted each member as he or she came in. As he shook hands and made small talk, Barry was reminded of how much he really loved these people and how sure he believed his call to pastor them to be. He felt a few butterflies as the board took their seats around the table, but they were from anticipation, not anxiety.

Jim opened the meeting with prayer and then grudgingly, it seemed, turned the meeting over to Barry. Barry ignored Jim's dour expression, smiled and thanked him, and began to speak.

"When I became the pastor of this church, folks, I came in here thinking that I knew what you wanted, but I never stopped to ask what you needed. That was a very big mistake, and for that I asked your forgiveness."

Barry looked into the eyes of each person around the table, sure that he now had their undivided attention.

"I was—am—a young pastor with a lot to learn. Many of you are much wiser than me in the ways of this congregation; many of you know much more than I do. Which makes it all the more unfortunate that I came in thinking I knew exactly what we needed to do to reach our community. I am sorry for that, and I pledge that I will do a better job as your pastor and as your representative to our community."

Barry paused to let that sink in, again meeting each person's eyes.

"I am almost done dwelling on all of the things I could have done differently. What is more important now are the tasks we face moving forward. And as I see them, those tasks require that we first ask some questions about our identity as a church, who we really are as opposed to what we aspire to be or imagine ourselves to be. I believe that every time a group experiences a problem, it is because that group is aware of a gap between how things are and how they want things to be."

Barry brushed a lock of hair from his eyes and continued. "That sounds pretty elementary, and it is. But many times, groups ignore the fact that they are all in it together. Instead of honestly confronting the gap and deciding how to close it, the group sometimes looks to deny that gap in any way possible but splits into warring factions or tries to find a superstar to solve all of their problems. And you all have figured out that I am no superstar." At this last comment, the group laughed together. Barry sensed he was forging a connection between him and the group.

"A writer I really like by the name of Jim Collins says that when an organization does something really important, the first thing it must do is to 'confront the brutal facts.' And that's what we need to do here. The main fact to confront is this gap between where we are and where we want to be. Once we define that, we will need to define what kind of change it will take to close the gap. And then we will have to decide whether we are willing to pay the sometimes high costs of change."

Barry paused. "Before I go further, are there any thoughts you all have?"

Halfway down the table, Kim James cleared her throat. "I am speaking for no one else when I say this, so please, no one get defensive." She smiled and continued. "As I have been thinking about things at the church, it has occurred to me that I often want things to change, but I don't want to change myself. My ideal is to have needed change occur without personally changing in ways that may be uncomfortable. That's all."

Around the table there were one or two chuckles as individuals saw themselves in Kim's words.

Barry jumped back in. "Kim, I appreciate your saying that because it is true for all of us, even those of us who are trying to engineer change! I can not only empathize with you but I can relate."

Barry was silent for a few moments to allow others to speak. When no one did, he continued.

"I think those fundamental tasks—confronting the brutal facts by identifying the gap between our reality and our ideal, measuring what it would take to close that gap, and then choosing whether to accept the necessary change—should be our focus now. I think we should talk less about peripheral items, because those things tend to cause petty quarrels and distract us from the real challenges we face.

"I need to emphasize as well that I don't have all the answers. I don't know yet where we should go. I have come to question the conventional wisdom that vision is given to a pastor and then his job is to rally leaders and the congregation to support the vision. I now believe that vision is given to the people of a congregation and that my job as a pastor is to draw that vision out, clarify it, and then champion it. And the best way for me to begin that process is to focus on asking the right questions, questions that revolve around values.

Questions such as, What is really important to us as a church? What is our unique mission, our singular purpose? What do we believe about how this church should engage with the community around us? How do we define the task of a leader here?

"Again, I don't have the answers. I believe that you do and that with God's help we will come to know what they are. I am confident that I can lead us in this process, and I am eager to do just that."

Barry had a few more things to say, but he paused again to glance around the table. "Yes, Terry?" he said, acknowledging a raised hand.

Terry Daley scratched his nose before speaking. "I guess I'm struggling a bit here. I like the way you define vision as being in the congregation rather than just transmitted from the pastor. But I also wonder then exactly how a pastor is supposed to lead. Is it just asking questions and facilitating our discussions? Surely there is more to it than that . . ." He looked at Barry with a silent appeal.

"Terry, I wish I had a hard and fast answer to that, but I don't. I know I need to do some internal work of my own to determine what I believe about that. I do know that the models I have seen and was taught are not adequate anymore. And I also know I will need input from all of you on that. I believe that for now I should continue to pastor, counsel, and preach. And I am going to lead this board with open hands but with energy as we define who we are and the role we are to play in reaching out to our community. My job is to focus us on questions about the core values and beliefs we hold together and how those values can play out in our life together. I am tremendously humbled and excited to get to do that together with you."

Barry leaned back in his chair and smiled at the group. "Some of you may want more answers than I can give now, more answers than I think any of us can give now. I don't have them yet. Over the next months, our focus at these board meetings will become wrestling with these core issues together. We will find answers together, and it is my great honor to be your pastor and leader at this great time for our church."

Barry looked around the room again, saw that no one was wanting to speak, and so glanced at Jim to turn the meeting back over to him. It was at that moment that Barry realized he had never been in a meeting in which Jim did not dominate or even speak. Jim had been silent, and Barry wasn't sure what to make of that.

Jim didn't exactly look happy, but he didn't look hostile either, much to Barry's relief. Actually, he looked a bit puzzled, but he pulled himself together to close the meeting.

Barry gathered up his folders and papers and was saying goodnight to a few of the board members when he glanced toward the doorway and saw Jim standing there. Their eyes locked for a moment. Barry saw something new in Jim's eyes. Not affection or trust, to be sure, but something that perhaps could be the beginning of a grudging respect. It was good enough for Barry, for now.

Jim looked Barry dead in the eye, gave a short nod, turned around, and headed for his car.

CHAPTER 9

Entrusted

S o it went a little smoother than you expected?" Elliott said.

Barry, seated once again in the comfortable brown couch in Elliott's study, nodded. "There was no clear resolution or massive rush of support, mind you. No one lifted me on their shoulders and carried me out of the room calling me the greatest pastor of all time," Barry said with a laugh. "But even though there is a long row to hoe, I thought I sensed a softening in the room last night. And, of course, Jim's reaction . . . he was hard to read, but something was definitely different with him."

"Ah, yes, Jim," Elliott said thoughtfully. "We should talk for just a few moments about Jim. Of all the things you told me about last night's meeting, the thing that seems most significant to me is that Jim somehow ceased to be the spokesman for the group."

"I noticed that too," Barry replied. "He didn't speak much at all. What do you think was behind that?"

"I suspect," said Elliott, "that last night marked the crucial moment when the members of the board, at least some of them, began to think rather than to react. As an adaptive leader, you have required action and thought just by asking the right questions. The questions were the right ones because they are complex and because they call on each person to participate in the process. A group will always need leaders, but this one will not need a dominant spokesperson anymore."

"Makes sense," said Barry. "I have to tell you too, Elliott, that my own heart seems to have softened some toward Jim. It's not that I trust him yet, and to be honest I really don't like or enjoy him as a person, but I do feel a degree of empathy for him that I haven't felt before."

"I was hoping to hear you say that at some point, Barry." Elliott took another sip of coffee from his blue pottery mug. "Now that you are beginning to understand yourself at a deeper level, you will increasingly have the ability to understand others and to be more empathetic with them. You will become a better, more compassionate pastor in part because you have become more compassionate for yourself. Now, I know you don't like that kind of language and you feel it is self-absorbed, but I am going to let it stand anyway. Indulge an older guy!

"There is something I would like to ask you, though, Barry," Elliott continued. "How do you view Jim now?"

Barry thought for a few moments. He wanted to choose his words carefully and to ensure that what he said was authentic.

"As I said, I still do not enjoy him as a person. I don't consider him a friend or an ally, though I can envision a future in which we might be partners with a good working relationship. I think he is a man who has accomplished a reasonable amount in his life but has not accomplished all that he would have liked. He sees maybe twenty years of life left for him, and twenty years seems a lot shorter than it did earlier in his life. He is wondering what kind of legacy he will leave, and to him it looks grim. He is afraid that at the end, his life will not have mattered much.

"He sees the church as a place where he can leave a mark. He has loved and sacrificed for the church but is smart enough to know that it has declined significantly. At some level, he feels some guilt for that. But his response has been to try harder to make the church work. Like a lot of us men, his response when he feels something slipping out of his control is to tighten whatever control he does have.

"He accuses me of being controlling, and there is probably some truth in that. But he is mostly Red Zoning on the issue of control, because that is his deal. He sees my influence in setting a new direction as a symbol of his own failure. He knows change needs to happen, but he also wants to play a key role in that. So he is torn."

Elliott sat still, very impressed and even moved. "Barry, I am struck by the wisdom and empathy in your words. Your relationship with Jim will have ups and downs in the days ahead, but now you are prepared to handle those as a pastor and leader without Red Zoning.

"We are all flawed. You have learned this deeply, Barry. You have come to understand your own flaws and some of the reasons behind them. And once a person comes to that point, they are free not to react to the flaws of another. This is living purely in the Blue Zone. When we understand our own flaws and can be empathetic about the flaws of others, we have the freedom to be a Blue Zone leader, who can see the flaws of others while at the same time embracing and supporting a flawed person.

"And after embracing the person, we are free to be a wise, adaptive leader. When a person is at their most oppositional, that is the time when they are most vulnerable. Instead of ignoring or attempting to overwhelm this resistance, we are free to see it as our ally, by not responding the way we normally would. This is the sacred moment when transformation can occur, when a person is most vulnerable. If they are supported instead of being ignored or opposed, the resisting person can move toward the Blue Zone.

"And this is the moment when the pastor becomes a healer, a pastor who heals himself or herself, other individuals, and even whole congregations. That is the Blue Zone pastor. And, Barry, I believe down in my bones that this is the kind of pastor you are now becoming. I wish I could tell you how humble and grateful and happy this makes me."

For many moments, the two men—now friends—sat in companionable silence.

Finally, Elliott stood up and walked over to his window. With his back to Barry, he said "You know, my friend, that our relationship changes today, don't you?"

"What do you mean, Elliott?" Barry asked, a little nervously.

"I mean that the pupil now becomes the teacher. You don't need me anymore. You are now free to move into your own destiny as a Blue Zone adaptive leader and to mentor others in this process as well. My great joy will be in watching you do that.

"Don't hear me wrong, Barry. We are friends for life and I will always be here for you, and I will even be here for friends of yours, if you would like. But it is your time now, your time to live the life as a pastor you were meant to live, to lead your congregation wisely and well, and to encourage other pastors to live the same way by practicing the principles we have discovered together."

"Come on, Elliott," Barry exclaimed. "You are too humble! I discovered these principles; you already knew them."

"It is not that simple," Elliott replied. "Every time I help someone else to discover these principles—whether that person is in business, social service, government, or in your case, ministry—I discover them again for myself."

After another pause, Barry spoke again. "Elliott, I accept your charge. You will never know how much you have meant to me and to my family and what you will mean to this church and to those with whom I may be privileged to share these principles along the way. I want to ask you a final mentoring question. If you had to summarize the things you have helped me to see, how would you do that?"

Elliott turned away from the window to face Barry. He smiled gently. "Barry, would you make my joy complete by summarizing these things yourself?"

"Yes, Elliott, I will try. First, even though we call these principles, they are not an easy, superficial list. I believe you have taught me mysteries as well as factual statements. In many ways, I have more questions than answers, except I think my questions are better, more substantive ones now. To be honest, I see my life's path less in a cut and dried way. I don't know what my life and ministry will bring. I do feel that I have new lenses to view life through and the tools I need for the journey.

"My faith in God precedes everything, of course. My relationship with Christ is elemental. But the new tools I have include understanding what it means to be a Blue Zone leader. I have the tool of distinguishing between technical and adaptive change, and a map to becoming an adaptive leader. Another tool is understanding that resistance is my ally and knowing how to mobilize resistance into a force that unifies and heals. You have given me many more tools, but these are the ones that immediately come to mind."

"I have one more tool I want to give you as you leave, Barry." With those words, Elliott slipped a piece of parchment paper into Barry's hands.

Barry picked up his coat, slipped the paper into its pocket, and the two men walked to the front door.

"Let's have lunch together soon, Barry," Elliott said as he held the door open. "And this time, you pick up the check!"

The two men embraced, Barry fighting his emotions and finally losing the battle, to a degree.

Five minutes into his journey, Barry could stand it no more. He pulled off at a side street, put the car in park, and pulled the piece of parchment paper from his coat and spread it out on the seat next to him.

The paper contained a prayer of monk and spiritual writer Thomas Merton, printed in beautiful calligraphy. With the words of the prayer in his head, Barry drove home.

MY LORD GOD, I have no idea where I am going. I do not see the road ahead of me. I cannot know for certain where it will end. Nor do I really know myself, and the fact that I think that I am following your will does not mean that I am actually doing so. But I believe that the desire to please you does in fact please you. And I hope I have that desire in all that I am doing. I hope that I will never do anything apart from that desire. And I know that if I do this, you will lead me by the right road, though I may know nothing about it. Therefore will I trust you always, though I may seem to be lost and in the shadow of death. I will not fear, for you are ever with me, and you will never leave me to face my perils alone.

RESPONSE ACTIVITIES

PHASE 1

The Problem Is You,
So Know Yourself

O ne of Jesus' more profound statements concerns speck-gazing—picking out a speck in another's eye while ignoring the beam in one's own eye. Interesting how he turns the issue around. Most of our time is absorbed with looking at the offenses of another person. But it's our belief that the speck in the other's eye *is* the beam in my eye. When I judge the other person, I am in fact judging myself.

So the first step in proper conflict management is to understand ourselves.

In a survey published in *Your Church* magazine,[1] the following were revealed as reasons ministers leave the ministry or are pressured to resign:

- 46 percent left the ministry because of a conflict in vision between themselves and their church.
- 38 percent left because of personality conflicts with board members.
- 32 percent because of the unrealistic expectations placed on them.
- 24 percent because of a lack of clear expectations.
- 22 percent because of theological differences.

Eight years later, in a survey of 506 pastors who were readers of *Leadership* journal, 95 percent reported experiencing conflict.[2] When respondents were asked about the causes of conflict in the church, they reported the following sources:

---

1. John C. LaRue Jr., "Forced Exits: A Too-Common Ministry Hazard," *Your Church* 42, no. 2 (March/April 1996), 72.

2. Eric Reed, "Leadership Surveys Church Conflict," *Leadership* 25, no. 4 (fall 2004), 25–26.

- 85 percent: control issues
- 64 percent: vision/direction
- 43 percent: leadership changes
- 39 percent: pastor's style
- 33 percent: financial issues
- 23 percent: theology/doctrine
- 22 percent: cultural issues
- 16 percent: other

These ministers, however, reported not only negative outcomes but also positive outcomes:

Negative Outcomes of Conflict	Positive Outcomes of Conflict
68 percent: damaged relationships	72 percent: I'm wiser
58 percent: sadness	44 percent: purifying process
32 percent: decline in attendance	42 percent: better-defined vision
32 percent: leaders left the church	35 percent: better communication with congregation
31 percent: loss of trust	30 percent: stronger relationships
29 percent: bitterness	16 percent: reconciliation
3 percent: loss of communication with congregation	16 percent: growth in attendance

Ministers go into ministry because of a calling, a calling that includes changing lives. But after a few months, they become embroiled in conflicts that distract them from that call and make their lives miserable.

This conflict is not a personal failure, nor is it a distraction from their calling. It *is* their calling. But for most ministers, conflict is the result of a misunderstanding of the forces that are brought to bear as they struggle to lead their community.

In our story, Barry's life had spun out of control. He had left everything to attend seminary and then go into ministry. And what thanks did he get? One reason he's in a fix is because he doesn't understand the internal forces that are in play:

- The stories we tell about others are really stories about ourselves.
- None of us does a very good job of examining ourselves. It takes practice.
- The less one deals with his or her own story, the more it crops up, over and over, in the stories we now live.
- Conflict is never about the other person. It's always about me. Dealing with conflict teaches me about *me*.

Self-awareness allows you to be able to manage yourself. Once you are able to manage yourself, you are able to better understand relationships (and the conflicts that relationships always involve) and, as a consequence, to better manage relationships.

Work through the following exercises, which are designed to lead you to greater self-awareness.

Reflection Scenario and Questions

Think of a time in ministry when an idea or initiative you'd introduced was called into question, creating controversy. As the controversy escalated, every idea seemed to be challenged. You worked hard to understand the intensity of the pushback, only to find your best efforts challenged or dismissed.

1. At what point did you become aware that you were angry and resentful?

2. As you became aware of your anger, what did you do?

3. As you were challenged, at what point did you decide it was important to take a stand on or to bring a firm hand to the situation?

4. When you took a stand, did the problem resolve or escalate?

5. If the problem resolved, did those who were adversarial comply with your wishes?

6. Is compliance the same as commitment? Why or why not?

Red Zone, Blue Zone Quiz

Review for a moment the points that Elliott made to Barry regarding the Red and Blue Zones (chapters 2 and 3) by taking the following quiz.

THE RED ZONE, THE BLUE ZONE

Agree	Disagree	
❑	❑	1. Conflict and confrontation are the same.
❑	❑	2. Conflict in teams is good.
❑	❑	3. Lack of conflict in teams indicates high team cohesion.
❑	❑	4. Conflict in teams indicates poor leadership.
❑	❑	5. Conflict in teams should always be dealt with.
❑	❑	6. Conflict in teams should never be dealt with.
❑	❑	7. When conflict arises, it is the responsibility of the team leader to deal with it.
❑	❑	8. When conflict arises, it is the responsibility of the entire team to deal with it.
❑	❑	9. Expressed conflict in teams is less dangerous than unexpressed conflict.
		10. When I see conflict among my coworkers, I feel _____.

Issues regarding conflict are confusing. Is conflict good or bad? How do I manage it? As we have stated, conflict is necessary and beneficial, if it is focused properly (i.e., in the Blue Zone). As conflict strays away from issues and accesses personal stories (i.e., in the Red Zone), conflict becomes unmanageable and destructive.

The Red Zone is where the atmosphere is characterized by a lack of professionalism and by emotional heat, which can burn those who get too close.

When we focus more on feelings and personal issues than on results, people aren't sure where their personal and professional boundaries lie, and everyone is unsure of how to act. One of the classic Red Zone behaviors is blame-shifting, an unwillingness to accept that one is part of the problem. In the Red Zone, no one knows where they stand, what is expected of them, what is appropriate and inappropriate, or even whether they are doing a good job. That creates uncertainty and anxiety. And people generally don't know how to handle uncertainty and anxiety, so they lash out at others as the cause of their anxiety.

RED ZONE	BLUE ZONE
This conflict is personal.	This conflict is professional.
It's about me.	It's about the business.
Emotions rule without being acknowledged.	The mission of the organization rules.
I must protect myself because I'm feeling weak.	I must protect the team and the business.
I deny my emotions; therefore I project them onto others.	I understand and acknowledge my emotions.
The situation escalates.	The situation is reframed into a more useful construct.
Behaviors: · I disengage. · I become easily annoyed. · I am resentful. · I procrastinate. · I attack the other personally. · I use alcohol as medication. · I avoid people and situations.	Behaviors: · I am thoughtful. · I am reflective. · I listen for what the underlying issue might be. · I do not see negative intentions in the other person.

Your Red Zone Behaviors

Make a list of your Red Zone behaviors. You may find it helpful to photocopy this chart. You may want to make two separate lists (or three or four if you like), one for work and one for home (or church or club, etc.).

RED ZONE BEHAVIORS

As I sink into the Red Zone, my personal story emerges. That story typically has one of four central themes: Will I survive? Am I acceptable? Am I competent? Am I in control? Each time I sink into my Red Zone, this same core theme emerges. Consequently, you will hear me express the same theme over and over again. "You're trying to control me!" (control). "Don't you think I can do this?" (competence). This Red Zone theme will color my every interaction until I become aware of it and am able to manage it appropriately.

As my Red Zone core theme is activated, feelings associated with that issue are also activated. I then sink deeper into a morass of feelings, many of which come from old stories unrelated to the current story that has provoked my Red Zone response.

Which of the following describes you best?

RED ZONE THEMES

RED ZONE ISSUE	SELF-DESCRIPTION	POSITIVE SIDE	NEGATIVE SIDE
Survival	"I must take care of myself. The world is full of peril, so I must enjoy the moment."	People with this issue have traits of competence, self-reliance, and responsibility.	People with this issue lack the ability to trust others and tend to be wary and troubled in relationships. They have little interest in anything but what is of practical benefit. They become angry and panicky (Red Zone) whenever they feel their survival is threatened.
Acceptance	"I will do anything to be loved and accepted by others. I want to please people."	People with this issue have a heart for serving others and are attentive to the needs and feelings of other people.	People with this issue are overly compliant and self-effacing. They tend to be rescuers. They become angry and carry personal grudges (Red Zone) whenever they feel they have been rejected.

Control	"The world is a threatening place, and the only way I can feel safe is if I control every situation and the people around me."	People with this issue tend to have strong leadership qualities. They are vigilant, highly organized, and have high expectations of themselves.	People with this issue often wall themselves off emotionally. They do not let others get too close to them. They can be overly controlling of others— bossy, directive, demanding, rigid, and nitpicky. They impose perfectionist demands on others. They become anxious and angry (Red Zone) whenever anyone or anything threatens their control.
Competence	"I am loved only on the basis of my performance. My performance is never good enough, so I never feel worthy of being loved."	People with this issue tend to be high achievers. If you are a leader, you want these people on your team, because they will work hard to achieve a great performance.	People with this issue are never satisfied with their achievements. They have a hard time receiving from other people. They impose perfectionist demands on themselves. They are defensive and easily angered (Red Zone) whenever they perceive that their competence is being questioned.

RESPONSE ACTIVITY 4

Boundaries

oundary issues go hand in hand with Red Zone issues. As I sink deeper into the Red Zone, my personal boundaries invariably are involved, and I engage others in my emotional drama in unhealthy ways.

Boundaries are the fences, both physical and emotional, that mark off our world, creating zones of safety, authority, privacy, and territoriality. Boundaries are essential components because they:

- Define who we are, what we believe, think, feel, and do, and where our story ends and others' begins.
- Restrict access and intrusions.
- Protect priorities.
- Differentiate between personal (Red Zone) and professional (Blue Zone) issues.

For some people, boundaries become too rigid. When this occurs, there is a bottleneck in the flow of vital information that is the lifeblood of any healthy person. Stylized ways of behaving become fixed. Prejudices are constructed and maintained.

For other people, boundaries become too porous or ambiguous. In such cases, the integrity and cohesion of the person are threatened by a lack of definition: "Who am I, other than an extension of you?"

We are used to the visible boundary markers of our world: fences, hedges, traffic signs. Less obvious, but equally effective, are the internal boundaries that mark off emotional territory: "These are my thoughts, my feelings, my story" or "This is my responsibility, not yours." These internal boundaries are emotional barriers that protect and enhance the integrity of individuals.

A person can be so closed-minded that no new thoughts or information can reach her. She can also be so open-minded that she's swayed by every idea that comes along, never able to establish her own position on anything.

Boundaries are critical in understanding the Red Zone, because among other things, sinking into the Red Zone represents a boundary violation. When I'm in conflict with another person, it is critical that my thoughts and emotions stay present to the issues upon which we disagree. When I permit old storylines to color my feelings, I violate a boundary. When I begin to see the other person as someone other than who she truly is, I violate a boundary. For those people who have poor boundaries (too rigid or too porous), the dangers of Red Zoning are more prominent.

Here's a quick test to help you determine the health of your personal boundaries.[3] See if you agree or disagree with the following statements.

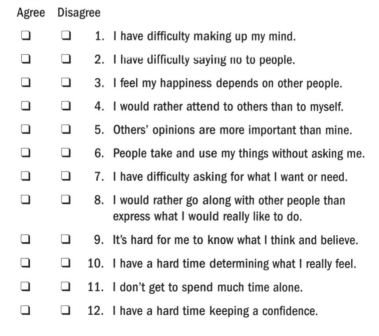

Agree	Disagree		
❏	❏	1.	I have difficulty making up my mind.
❏	❏	2.	I have difficulty saying no to people.
❏	❏	3.	I feel my happiness depends on other people.
❏	❏	4.	I would rather attend to others than to myself.
❏	❏	5.	Others' opinions are more important than mine.
❏	❏	6.	People take and use my things without asking me.
❏	❏	7.	I have difficulty asking for what I want or need.
❏	❏	8.	I would rather go along with other people than express what I would really like to do.
❏	❏	9.	It's hard for me to know what I think and believe.
❏	❏	10.	I have a hard time determining what I really feel.
❏	❏	11.	I don't get to spend much time alone.
❏	❏	12.	I have a hard time keeping a confidence.

---

3. Based on ideas suggested by C. L. Whitfield, *Boundaries and Relationships* (Deerfield Beach, FL: Health Communications, 1993).

❑ ❑ 13. I am very sensitive to criticism.

❑ ❑ 14. I tend to stay in relationships that are harmful to me.

❑ ❑ 15. I tend to take on or feel what others are feeling.

❑ ❑ 16. I feel responsible for other people's feelings.

If you answered "agree" to even two or three of these statements, you have at least some issues with porous boundaries. The more statements you agree with, the greater your problem. If this is the case, you're having trouble knowing where your story ends and others' stories begin.

Now let's see if your boundaries might be too rigid.

Agree Disagree

❑ ❑ 1. My mind is always made up.

❑ ❑ 2. It is much easier for me to say no to people than to say yes.

❑ ❑ 3. My happiness never depends on other people.

❑ ❑ 4. I would rather attend to myself than to others.

❑ ❑ 5. My opinion is more important than others'.

❑ ❑ 6. I rarely, if ever, lend my things to other people.

❑ ❑ 7. Most issues appear very black and white to me.

❑ ❑ 8. I know exactly what I think and believe on almost every issue.

❑ ❑ 9. I have a hard time determining what I really feel.

❑ ❑ 10. I spend much time alone.

❑ ❑ 11. I keep most of my thoughts to myself.

❑ ❑ 12. I am immune to criticism.

❑ ❑ 13. I find it difficult to make and maintain close relationships.

❑ ❑ 14. I never feel responsible for other people's feelings.

If you agreed with two or three of these statements, your boundaries are probably too rigid.

Gaps and Overlaps

Boundary problems always arise at the extremes, where boundaries are either too vague and weak or too rigid. Rigid boundaries produce gaps, and weak boundaries produce overlaps.

The establishment of boundaries can also be paradoxical—not an either-or proposition when it comes to rigidity or permeability. Those with permeable boundaries often will compensate by establishing extremely rigid boundaries.

My Role versus My Self

A confusion that continues to arise with clergy is the distinction between my role as clergy, and my self (who I am as a person). Barry has had great difficulty with this, not realizing that much of the resistance from his board had to do with his role as clergy, not an attack on his person. However, as Barry misunderstands, then mishandles the accusations, the attacks become personal.

So much of what the pastor deals with, both positive ("You're simply the best pastor we've ever had!") and negative ("You're constantly trying to control our meetings, and I resent it"), has to do with the role of pastor. Bound up in this role are ideas of parent, authority figure, healer, disciplinarian, and a whole host of others. Congregants transfer their leftover ideas and feelings from parents and other authority figures onto the pastor. Hence, the pastor is either overly adored ("I know you will be able to heal all of my childhood wounds") or reviled ("I can't believe you would be such an uncaring cad"), according to his or her role as pastor. This is what makes so many of the attacks that pastors suffer seem so disproportionate and illogical.

PHASE 2

Resistance Is Your Ally

The book of James begins with this compelling statement: "When all kinds of trials and temptations crowd into your lives, my brothers, don't resent them as intruders, but welcome them as friends!" (Phillips). When Barry walked into the board meeting that fateful night and realized that a kangaroo court awaited him, the last thing on his mind was embracing this pressure as a friend. The board members were armed with their accusations—watered-down sermons, trivial expenditures, weird new approaches to worship. And besides, Barry is new at this pastoring thing, and basically doesn't know what he is doing. All in all, there is a whole lot of resistance to Barry's leadership.

In any organization, voices of dissent provide clues about unexpressed pain within the organization. However, these voices are often misinterpreted by the leaders of the organization because they are seen as oppositional. It is hard to hear the message when one feels personally attacked, and almost any response to the attack makes the situation worse. However, as we shall see, it is precisely at these critical moments, when resistance arises, that you, the leader, are in a pivotal position to bring about change.

Answer the following questions to get a sense of how you have handled difficult situations in the past. Then in the following pages, you will find clear guidelines for managing yourself (staying Blue Zone) as you navigate the turbulent waters of church leadership.

RESPONSE ACTIVITY 5
Reflection Scenario and Questions

Think of a time when you knew that a controversy was brewing and you worked hard to avoid it. Reflect on who was involved, what the issues were, and how you began to mobilize internally.

1. Did you fear that things would get out of control with the controversy?
2. Did you fear the outcome would not be what you wanted?
3. How did you try to defuse the situation (e.g., controlling the conversation)?
4. What toll did this take on you?
5. How often do you work to avoid a conflict?

Resistance. Pushback. Call it what you will. It's basically an opposing force that slows or stops movement. Pastors of churches must come to expect it. Most people, after ministering for a time, do expect it, but they also resent it and see it as harmful. "How dare he question my leadership!"

A critical principle to keep in mind: the success of every church initiative, every new program, or the hiring of every staff member hinges on the moment when resistance emerges. Never be surprised that resistance has emerged, no matter how much homework you've done prior to taking action. It will emerge. Welcome it! And then handle it correctly.

All of us from time to time resist. It's a way of protecting ourselves from real or perceived danger. In and of itself, it is not a bad thing. It's merely energy. You've probably already noted in ministry that it especially emerges when change looms. If we can effectively redirect that energy, we can move the resistance in the direction of change. Resistance can take on many guises:

- *Confusion.* "So why are we doing this?" (Asked after many explanations.)

- *Immediate criticism.* "What a dumb idea."
- *Denial.* "I don't see any problem here."
- *Malicious compliance.* "I concur completely and wholeheartedly."
- *Sabotage.* "Let's get him!"
- *Easy agreement.* "No problem."
- *Deflection.* "What do you think the Cubs' chances are this year?"
- *Silence.*
- *In-your-face criticism.* "You're the worst pastor we've ever had!"[4]

---

4. Adapted from Rick Maurer, *Beyond the Wall of Resistance* (Austin, TX: Bard Books, 1996).

Resistance

Take a moment to think of resistances you have been dealing with, and fill out the chart on page 119.

When faced with resistance, we can act either in the Red Zone or in the Blue Zone. When we react in the Red Zone, we first assume that the resistance is about our persons, not our roles. Feeling personally attacked, we then:

- Use power.
- Manipulate those who oppose.
- Apply force of reason.
- Ignore the resistance.
- Play off relationships.
- Make deals.
- Kill the messenger.
- Give in too soon.

You can be sure that you're in the Red Zone with your responses when:

- They increase rather than decrease resistance.
- They fail to create synergy.
- They create fear and suspicion.
- They separate us from others.

So what to do? Remember, you must be in the Blue Zone. The first step in staying in the Blue Zone is to realize that the resistance has to do with my role as pastor, and it is therefore not about me personally. Then I can:

Maintain clear focus:
- Keep both the long and the short view—one eye on the goal, and one on the present moment.

- Persevere. Hang in there.

Embrace resistance (Remember, it's my ally!):
- Move toward the resistance. Remember, resistance always signals that the resistant person is expressing internal conflict. The voice of resistance tells you what's wrong. The most resistant person is merely the voice for others. Once you know why people are concerned, you can attempt to find common ground. Knowing objections unlocks possibilities.
- Hear the reasons beneath the reasons. People fear change.

Respect those who resist:
- Continually monitor your Red Zone.
- Listen with interest.
- Tell the truth.

Join with the resistance:
- Begin together.
- Look for ways that the situation needs to change.
- Find themes and possibilities. People polarize quickly around issues, with the Red Zone rising for all participants. Staying Blue Zone allows you to find paths to walk below the bluster and assist those who are in the Red Zone as they move toward the Blue Zone.

Who gives me the most resistance?	What form does that resistance take?	What is my normal response to this resistance?

Projection

There are aspects of myself that I have difficulty owning and dealing with. These aspects cause me anxiety. To reduce the anxiety, my mind keeps these aspects out of my awareness. Thus, my mind censors information that could be potentially troubling.

The buried unacceptable parts don't stay buried within me. Two things happen: 1) they covertly influence my behavior; 2) I project them onto other people so that I can see them in action.

These disowned aspects of myself then become some of the raw material of my story-telling, giving shape and substance to what my mind constructs. Thus, I'm back to boundary problems. Projection is a boundary problem; I'm unable to keep my own story within myself. I project that story onto other people and act according to that story, not according to what that other person is doing. Pastors are projection screens for the congregation. Everything they struggle with—good or bad—gets put on the pastor.

Things That I Disdain

There are things about me—personality traits, propensities, maybe even that part of myself that is creative—that were systematically covered up as I grew up. This took place because, frankly, my parents, families, friends, and society couldn't handle these things. It's not that these things were bad; they were just unacceptable for one reason or another. For this reason I came to be uncomfortable with, or even to disdain, these things.

Take, as an example, an athletic child growing up in a literary family. The child's athletic talents are often ignored or actively discouraged, and they are driven from the growing child's awareness. He still has an athletic bent but is unable to develop it.

If I am angry about something, and I don't want to feel or to handle that feeling, then I can unconsciously project it onto you. If you buy it, also unconsciously, and act it out by expressing it for me to others and also back to me, then I won't have to own and deal with my feelings of anger and resentment. If you express the anger I have projected onto you too much to others and to me, I will criticize and berate you.

A Quiz

Answers to this quiz will give you insights into aspects of yourself you might not be fully aware of.

1. What things really set me off and cause me to overreact?

2. Do I read other people's minds? Whose? When do I read them? What is occurring?

3. What do I fear the most? Rejection? Loss of control? Incompetence? Abandonment?

4. What people or things do I hate the most?

5. What characteristics do I find myself disliking in others, especially those of the same sex? Is there one person in my life that I really can't stand? What is it about him or her that sets me off?

6. What things do I know about myself that I try hard to keep hidden, even from those closest to me?

7. What things do I never do, even though doing them may benefit me?

8. What strengths do I have that, being preoccupied with them, may prevent me from being real and having fulfilling relationships (e.g., always caretaking others prevents me from caring for myself)?

9. What are the themes of my dreams? Who is doing what?

10. What do others say about me, especially those closest to me (spouse, friends, parents)? How am I perceived in the organization?

11. Think back on a recent hardship, a loss of something truly important to you (spouse, friendship, job, status). What issues emerged? What was said to you?

GUISES UNDER WHICH PROJECTION MAY APPEAR

Characteristic	Definition	Example	Possible Projected Material
1. All-or-nothing behavior	Seeing people, places, or things only one way	All men are brutes. Bosses can't be trusted.	I am a brute. I can't be trusted.
2. Strong "yuck" reaction	Revulsion and antagonism in reaction to others' behavior	I hate neediness.	I hate my own neediness.
3. Repetition, compulsion	Poor choices I make over and over	I keep getting into bad relationships.	I keep hoping someone will take care of me.
4. Limits in my behavior	What I *never* do, even though doing it may benefit me	Never confront. Never share.	I fear dealing with or confronting my issues.
5. Strengths in my own behavior	What strengths I have that, being preoccupied with them, may prevent me from being real and having fulfilling relationships	Always caretaking for others prevents me from caring for myself.	Hoping I will be cared for.
6. Resentment	Longstanding unresolved anger or bitterness	I resent him for ____.	I fear facing ____.

Adapted from C. L. Whitfield, *Boundaries and Relationships* (Deerfield Beach, FL: Health Communications, 1993), 92–93.

Transference

In transference, I experience a person in the present as though they were a parental figure from my past; I transfer problems that I had in that original relationship into my current relationships. I had a bad relationship with my father; I transfer my feelings about him onto you, the pastor.

In order to experience the present person as a past person, I must transfer to the present person my relationship to the past authority figure. Thus, I am unable to know the present person for who she truly is as a person. I see her as that past person, because I'm looking at the qualities of that person, not the qualities standing before me in the present person.

Actually, it starts out that I unconsciously see the pastor as the good parent, the one who will heal wounds left behind by my parents. So my expectations of the pastor are enormous (again, when I received especially bad parenting and still struggle with the results of this). This is the process that unfolded between Barry and his board. He thought that these dedicated people wanted him to rejuvenate their dying church. That was only part of it. They unconsciously wanted him to heal their woundedness.

When the pastor fails to heal all of these wounds (and it is certain that this will happen, especially with the deeply wounded in the congregation), I now see the pastor as the bad parent, and I glue all of my wounded feelings from childhood on the pastor. Thus, I am transformed from needy, dependent child to attacking monster.

The same process can also happen for the pastor. He can begin to look for approval and acceptance from members of the congregation. The pastor's personal story that he can't handle is brought to the parishioner to resolve or absolve. The pastor expects the parish to affirm and appreciate him for his sacrifice and service to them.

When they are dissatisfied and critical or take the pastor for granted, the pastor will either react in hurt or anger and isolate himself from them, or try to please all the more through performance.

Postures

L et's add another piece to the puzzle.

People seem to be genuinely perplexed when they get into disagreements, and their adversary gets more and more perturbed. "Why can't that jerk see my position on this matter?" we scream, never realizing that we are throwing gasoline on the fire at the very moment we want to lower the intensity and move to agreement.

Before we look at the steps involved in this, let's review the steps we have already established:

- When I see you do something, I reach into my story to attach meaning to what I'm seeing ("Oh, you're attacking me because you think I'm an incompetent boob"). At this point I may go Red Zone, my intensity increasing as I experience anxiety over what I think is occurring ("You're not just disagreeing with my proposal, you're saying that I'm incompetent").
- As I go Red Zone, my anxiety (intensity) increases (not necessarily noticeable but enough to alter my behavior) because of the energy pouring in from my past story.

Now let's consider the next steps:

- When I get anxious, I assume one of several postures that I have learned in the past. These postures help me hold my anxiety at bay.
- My anxiety is held at bay temporarily because I disguise from you (and, more often than not, from myself) my true Red Zone feelings. I refuse to let you know that I am feeling weak, vulnerable, afraid, unacceptable.
- Unfortunately, the only thing you notice is my posture. Seeing my posture activates your story, and you react to me

accordingly, never taking the time to get beneath my posture to see what is going on with me.

Now think of the posture that you assume when you become anxious. You may not realize it, but when you become anxious and move into the Red Zone, you have a posture you assume to deal with the anxiety. This posture conveys information to the other person. Your posture may temporarily lower your anxiety, but unfortunately it will also likely cause a response in your adversary that is the opposite of what you hope to achieve.

Am I Forwarding This Discussion, or Inciting to Riot?

When I've been in and out of conflict with the same adversary over time (spouse, boss, colleague), the pattern of conflict gets stylized. Each of us responds to the other in very predictable ways.

This has a bad side to it: it takes very little provocation to fall into the pattern, assume the requisite postures, and have at it.

It also has a good side to it: I've done the same thing over and over again. This isn't rocket science! I only need to figure out my part of the pattern and change it. Unfortunately, I'm usually too busy yelling, "You change!" to realize that it's up to me to do the changing.

Red Zone issues give rise to feelings associated with those issues. And once aroused, those feelings lead me to assume certain postures.

These postures become important in my unfolding relationships with people important to me.

Now look at the following table. See if you can identify the posture you assume when you get anxious and go Red Zone. We also included the Red Zone issue that often (but not exclusively) occurs with each of the postures; for example, competence-issue people often take a blaming stance.

All of us can employ all of these postures from time to time. But you probably employ one of these the most, especially when your anxiety is particularly high.

Posture	Hoped for Result	Your Insides	Others' Response
Placating (often used by Acceptance people)	So others won't be mad "Spare me."	"I feel like nothing inside."	Guilt
Blaming (often used by Controlling people)	So others will see me as strong "Obey me."	"I'm lonely and unsuccessful."	Fear
Computing (often used by Survival people)	So others will see I'm not threatened "Ally with me."	"I feel vulnerable."	Envy
Distracting (often used by Competence people)	So others will ignore the threat "Tolerate me."	"Nobody cares. There's no place for me."	Fun

Adapted from Virginia Satir, *Peoplemaking* (Palo Alto, CA: Science and Behavior, 1972).

PHASE 3
Adaptive Change

O nce a person has understood her Red Zone, come to terms with it, and been able to manage it effectively, she is able to establish more of a Blue Zone pattern of living and leading. And as Barry discovered in our story, she can begin to make critical distinctions between technical and adaptive changes.

Life, and certainly church life, has this annoying way of serving up problems that don't lend themselves to easy answers. Even so, people look to those in authority to deliver solutions. Unfortunately, pastors all too often are more than willing to assume these expectations. Instead of solving the problems, the pastor becomes the one upon whom the congregation can dump all of its ambivalence, anxiety, and anger.

An example is an established, aging congregation in a historic building in an ethnically changing neighborhood. What has developed is a gap between what people hope for ("I want my church to remain the same as it has been") and the present reality ("There is no way it can remain the same, with everything around it changing quickly"). Adaptive leadership for the pastor involves creating an environment in which the congregation can wrestle with the competing values and implications associated with this problem.

Technical change refers to fixes, such as altering techniques or acquiring new equipment or reshuffling personnel in an attempt to change the situation. These problems aren't trivial, but they do involve solutions already existing within organizations. Adaptive solutions involve a deeper level of change; they often require us to alter deeply held beliefs and modify established habits and patterns of behavior. It is those who are directly affected by the solutions who must be guided by the leader through the process of finding the solutions, no matter how painful this process might be.

The leadership failure that afflicts all too many organizations is the tendency to treat adaptive problems with technical solutions. When communication breaks down on a church staff, when churches become stuck and unable to establish their mission and vision for the future, or when Sunday morning worship attendance drops dramatically as the surrounding neighborhood undergoes cultural change, you generally have a major adaptive problem that needs far-reaching adaptive solutions. Mere technical patches and fixes will never work.

In the following pages, you will be taking a look at yourself as a leader. Work through the various scenarios and quiz yourself on how you have handled these situations in the past. Then we'll unpack the important concepts of adaptive and technical change.

RESPONSE ACTIVITY 10

The Adaptive Leader

Scenario 1

As the pastor, you are the authority figure in your church. Two of your staff members have asked you to resolve an interpersonal conflict between them. They tell you they will abide by whatever decision you make. Consider how you would answer the following questions.

What's your approach as an adaptive leader?

1. Do you help them resolve the issue?
2. Do you resolve it for them?
3. Do you believe they can resolve the issue?
4. Do you expect them to work at it until they resolve the issue themselves?

Scenario 2

As the pastor and leader of the church elders, you have agreed that decisions concerning the strategic focus of your church will be made by consensus. The group becomes deadlocked over an important issue.

What's your approach as an adaptive leader?

1. Do you allow the conflict in the group to continue?
2. Do you choose the direction you want and try to influence the members?
3. Do you decide to relieve the stress in the group and make the decision for them?
4. Do you help the group discern what the underlying values conflict really might be?

Scenario 3

After a particularly difficult meeting in which a decision was finally reached, several staff members approach you to complain about one member who often challenges the group's consensus. They do not clearly ask you to intercede, but their intent is clear.
What's your approach as an adaptive leader?

1. Do you agree with their assessment of the person?
2. Do you hope the conflict will pass?
3. Do you decide to schedule a coaching session with the individual?
4. Do you suggest to those complaining that they should raise the issue at the next team meeting and make an effort to resolve the issue?

Scenario 4

A small group of church leaders has always been very supportive of you. They have supported all the changes you have suggested and been instrumental in helping you accomplish your vision. One day they approach you about a concern and want your support for their cause. You are concerned because you think what they want may not be in the best interests of the church.
What's your approach as an adaptive leader?

1. Do you risk losing their support by disappointing them?
2. Do you decide to give them your support and hope for the best?
3. Do you raise your concerns about the endeavor with them?
4. Do you challenge them to find a better alternative?

Rate Yourself

As the pastor of the church, I am willing to take the risk and accept the consequences of exceeding my authority to make a decision that I think will be good for the community.

Never   Sometimes   Always

I am willing to provide feedback to any group member whose performance is getting in the way of their growth and development, even though the conversation may be uncomfortable for me.

Never   **Sometimes**   **Always**

These and many other everyday situations require leadership skills. Your ability to handle these situations in a positive and productive way will often determine how effectively your church will serve its members. As the pastor and leader, you are responsible for creating an environment in which people can grow and develop. It is the responsibility of leaders in all organizations, sacred and secular, to help the community they serve face its conflicts, heal its divisions, and find new ways to move forward together.

People tend to think that their leaders must be charismatic speakers or dynamic personalities to effectively lead them. They are quick to look for heroes to solve their most difficult problems, but effective leadership centers around mobilizing the individual, the group, and the community to address and resolve its conflicts. These are the skills of the adaptive leader.

Technical versus Adaptive Change

So how do we know which order of change is required—technical change or adaptive change? The key question we have to ask ourselves when faced with such a situation is this: Can I solve this situation with resources, or does the solution lie in changing people's values, attitudes, and habits? If it is the latter, then we must boldly shoulder the task of producing adaptive change.

One reason this is such a difficult challenge for leaders is that before we can encourage adaptive change in others, we must accept adaptive change within ourselves. Like the people who work in our organization, we are creatures of fixed attitudes, beliefs, habits, and behavior patterns. We don't enjoy change any more than the people who work around us do. But that is the burden of leadership: to face facts, accept the truth about ourselves and our situation, to make internal adaptations of our own minds and emotions, and then to mobilize the people around us to adapt as well.

Make a list of key adaptive changes you have personally had to make in the course of your life. (Examples: Coming to faith. Career-path change.)

Adaptive change is not easy for anyone. In fact, it is extremely stressful and painful for everyone—for leaders and followers alike. It means releasing old beliefs, while adopting new beliefs, roles, relationships, attitudes, and behaviors. There is always resistance to adaptive change. Always. Old traditions, attitudes, habits, and comfort zones die hard. Disorientation and confusion are frequent by-products of adaptive change. Conflicts easily arise—and leadership must resist the temptation to merely suppress conflict instead of allowing those conflicts to bring important issues to the fore. Conflict and collective pain can often be useful in underscoring the need for adaptive change.

During times of adaptive change, it is crucial for leadership to maintain poise, exude confidence, quell fears, and hold a steady course. This means that leaders need to possess a high tolerance for uncertainty, frustration, and distress, both within themselves and in the people around them. During times of adaptive change, leadership will be scrutinized by followers, watching for both verbal and nonverbal signs of security and steadiness. Leadership must continually communicate assurance and confidence that the change is manageable, healthy, and for the betterment of everyone involved.

Make a list of adaptive changes your church has had to make in the last ten years.

Make a list of adaptive changes that your church will need to make in the next five years. Then prioritize your list, number 1 being the adaptive change that will need to be made first. For example:

1. Reach out to the growing Hispanic community.
2. Alter worship service to accommodate potential new members.

RESPONSE ACTIVITY 12

Reframing

People don't like to be in the dark, not knowing what's going on. We constantly search for meaning in everything we see and experience. When a person does something, we want to know their motivation and intent. "Why did he do that?"

Unfortunately, often our frames miss the mark. We say someone or something is bad or distasteful or rude, when in fact another explanation is more valid. At the same time, we assign intention to actions. "She did that because she wanted to hurt me, plain and simple!"

So where do these frames come from? They come from the stories we've stored in our heads, stories replete with heroes and villains, rescuers, and saints. And we project onto others all of those distasteful parts of ourselves that we can't look at and deal with. So if I have trouble with my powerful part and shrink from leadership, I might then project this onto others and see people constantly trying to control me. That becomes my frame in situation after situation.

As we place people around us into the stories we carry in our heads, and subsequently frame them, we are at the same time valuing these people, situations, and experiences. "Judy is such an asset to this company. She's always smiling and happy. Harry, on the other hand, is a lazy bum who constantly procrastinates." People then get forced into categories in our minds. Once a frame is established, it is very difficult to escape from it.

The goal of reframing is to change our perspective, the way we think about ourselves and our problems and other people—the way we act, relate, and feel.

THE FACT	THE FRAME
He comes in late to work a lot.	He's a lazy bum.
She disobeyed.	She is a bad person.
He ignored me.	He is insensitive.

She tells jokes.	**She is funny.**
He spoke with a loud, harsh voice.	**He is a tyrant.**

All behavior has numerous strains of motivation. Our tendency is to pick out only certain strains of motivation—our projections. Reframing picks out another, equally valid strain of motivation that sheds new light on the person or experience.

- "He did act poorly, but I think he did it to protect you."
- "She ignored you, but it might be because she's so shy and not because she's arrogant."
- "He spoke harshly, but it may be because he feels his authority is threatened, not because he's mean."

When I successfully change the meaning of a person or experience, my emotional response to that person or experience changes, and my behavior toward that person changes.

Exercise

In the left column of the table on page 137, write the various problems you have heard people express to you over the years (problems with themselves and others). In the right column, write a reframing of the problem.

Now think of some people in your life who are irritating, people who just send you over the edge (see p. 138). For example:

PERSON	HOW I SEE THE PERSON	REFRAMING
My boss	Micromanaging	Concerned about excellence
	Overbearing	Willing to take charge
	Devious	Clever

You don't necessarily have to buy the reframing at this point. The intent of this exercise is to begin to see other possibilities in this person's behavior.

PROBLEM	REFRAMING

PERSON	HOW I SEE THE PERSON	REFRAMING

Successful Reframing

Let's look at the elements of reframing. Putting this skill in your Blue Zone toolbox will enhance your ability to deal with people effectively. And of course, one must be *in* the Blue Zone to effectively implement reframing. To begin with, effective reframing:

1. *Provides an alternative view.* Remember, behavior has many motivational strains. It's always problematic to say that a person does a particular behavior for one particular reason. We usually pick the reason a person behaves a certain way from our own story (projection), and that makes it doubly problematic. Reframing provides another view.

2. *Is valid.* Reframing is not just picking reasons for behavior out of the blue. The reason picked for the reframing must be valid.

3. *Provides a positive option.* So many of the frames we impose on others are negative. Even when people do a nice thing (Mary decides to help build a Habitat for Humanity house), the frame is negative (Mary's only doing this to make herself look good in the community).

4. *Allows someone to take action.* As we apply negative frames to people, we often paralyze them, giving them no room to maneuver. If I constantly tell my son that he is lazy and insolent, that definition hems him in to behavior that fits the bill.

That's a problem seen over and over again with parents and with spouses. They've applied the same frame over and over to their kids or their spouse, frames that have served to define the person.

"You're just a no-good, worthless bum."
"You'll never amount to anything."
"You're a tireless nag."
"You're just looking out for yourself."

Each of these frames depletes a person's motivation and steals their energy for useful action.

Principles for Managing Conflict

We've established that conflict can be a good thing, a useful thing, and an indispensable thing. We've also argued that to make conflict work for us, there has to be in place certain prerequisites, the most important of which is our ability to monitor ourselves. Let's add another indispensable piece.

Walking hand in hand with conflict is caring. Wait just a minute! you say. Conflict and caring going together? How can that be? I'm in conflict when I'm angry, not when I feel warmth. If I care about someone, I can't be in conflict with them, or I'll hurt them. Right?

Well, no. Conflict that's useful, that calls out new information and understanding, and that leads to resolution is conflict that weds care for relationship with care for the achievement of goals. I don't have to sacrifice my relationship with you in order to achieve the ends that I'm passionate about. In fact, Blue Zone living allows me to set aside my own story, and all the baggage that that involves, and truly care about others, even in the midst of conflict.

Anita is a woman of principle who takes stands on issues, who is passionate about things she believes in. She's the pastor of a medium-sized mainline church in one of our nation's leading cities. She is well trained and knows what she's doing. Anita is also a person who cares deeply about her peers, her subordinates, and her superiors.

Because Anita generally operates in the Blue Zone, and has come to grips with her story and how it can contaminate relationships if she's not careful, she is able to enter into conflict with the denominational authorities, with fellow clergy, with her board, and with members of the congregation without any of these people feeling personally attacked.

Quite the contrary, to be in conflict with Anita is to know two things: 1) I am valued by her, and 2) she's going to fight me tooth and nail for things she believes to be right. She is a person who cares deeply about personal relationships and personal goals. Let's put this in a table.

CARING ABOUT THE RELATIONSHIP	CARING ABOUT THE ISSUE
· You personally, and our relationship, are important to me.	· I care very deeply about this issue on which we disagree.
· I really want to hear what you have to say.	· I want to clearly express my point of view on this matter.
· I respect your position.	· My position differs from yours.
· I will stay with this discussion until we reach an understanding.	· Please keep working with me until we reach an understanding.

Adapted from David Augsburger, *Caring Enough to Confront* (Ventura, CA: Regal, 1973), 59–61.

We've studied Anita and people just like her to find out what makes them tick. How can they stand firm, be passionate, and fight like mad, and yet never seem to alienate the people with whom they fight?

Congruent Living

We haven't spoken much of the role of communication in conflict. And it is a critical role. Communication not only transmits thoughts and ideas from one person to another, it also reveals things about the communicator (often that the speaker is unaware of) and conveys whether the speaker is in the Red Zone or the Blue Zone.

Our brains have different areas that are critical to communication, and that send and receive messages in different ways. Let's consider just two channels for communication.

The left side of the brain produces and processes words. It's the side that uses language. Here concepts are strung together and understood. Here the world is broken down into components. This is the side we usually think of when we think of communication.

The right side of the brain works completely different. It works in the shadows, somewhat out of our awareness. This side of the brain sends and receives messages concerning the relationship. It is the side of the brain where Red Zone behavior emerges.

Consider the two speakers Maurice and Art in the figure. Maurice (the speaker) has a particular intent as he speaks to Art. He wants Art to attend a special corporate meeting. That is the content of his message.

Notice that the impact on Art is totally different from Maurice's intention. Art has evidently gone Red Zone. The goal of communication is to have our intent equal the impact on our hearer. So what misfires?

We know a lot about content messages. We deal with words-formed-into-sentences every day. Relationship messages are formed by our bodies as we speak and are shaped by the context in which our messages are found. These messages tend to be sent and received outside of our awareness. So while Maurice is asking Art to go to the board meeting, Maurice's body is also sending messages, messages that state the nature of the relationship between Maurice and Art.

Because relationship messages are shaped outside of our awareness, they tend to have more power. We don't sit down and think about how we want these messages to be; they just emerge automatically.

We both send and receive relationship messages outside of awareness. So critical relationship messages are constantly being passed back and forth between us unconsciously. But the fact that we aren't aware of these messages doesn't mean that we don't act on them. We act on them all the time, reacting to insignificant comments as though the world were ending, blowing up when someone makes a simple request, steering clear of certain people because we just don't feel right around them.

Of course, these relationship messages are breeding grounds for Red Zone behaviors.

Secrets to Healthy Conflict

- Remember, the ability to manage conflict in a healthy way begins with you. So you need to ask yourself:

  - Do I understand my story, the themes that emerge from it, and the ways in which I still live it?

  - Am I comfortable with both my loving feelings and with my feelings of annoyance and frustration?

  - Do I respond flexibly to life's events?

  - Do I focus on issues and the task at hand (goal-directed)?

- Work with more rather than less information. Conflict in the Blue Zone deals with issues. To deal with issues effectively in the Blue Zone requires information from every reliable source available. If the conflict isn't personal, you can gather the information you need to make an informed decision.

- Debate on the basis of facts. Once you get the information you need, fight all you want. But the fight has to be about the facts, not about personalities.

- Develop multiple alternatives to enrich the level of debate. As the fight unfolds, generate a number of alternatives and write them down.

- Share commonly agreed-upon goals. Make sure everyone in the conflict shares the same goals.

- Inject humor into the decision-making process. The ability to laugh at a situation is the best signal that everyone is still in the Blue Zone (at least, if you're not laughing at someone). It also clears the air and lets everyone keep perspective ("This isn't so important that we can't still laugh").

- Maintain a balanced power structure. Nothing stops conflict faster than a power play. "I'm the boss. No more discussion. You'll do as I say." If that's the way you feel, then why invite alternative positions and get into conflict in the first place?

- Resolve issues without forcing unanimity. Forget total agreement. It's a pipe dream. More than that, if you have unanimity, you've probably got group-think on your hands, in which everyone puts their minds on hold and just votes with the majority.

Having trouble with some of these? It may be that the Red Zone is creeping into your ability to manage conflict appropriately.

The Confrontation Process

onflict often involves confrontation. We have all come across behavior that demands to be confronted. In fact, to allow certain behavior to go unchallenged is an affront to the organization.

All of us, from time to time, need to be confronted. We tend to excuse behavior that is unacceptable. At these times, we need a person who cares for us to confront us and direct us down the proper path. But if this is not done in a caring manner, our inclination is to dismiss the confronter as punitive and misguided. So when you confront:

- *Be honest and direct.*
- *Be specific.* Never generalize, because when you generalize, your story can come creeping back in, contaminating what you are trying to say.
- *Use I messages, not you messages.* We tend to confront with *you* messages. "You didn't do this right. You screwed up!" But such messages convey blame, making the confronted person defensive. When we use *I* messages, we own our responsibility, feelings, and demands without blaming.
- *Affirm in public; correct in private.* There is nothing more destructive to a person's dignity and to the morale of an organization than public confrontation. Affirmation is for the ears of the public. But correction should take place in privacy, and even then, correction should be within the context of care for and support of the person being corrected.
- *Distinguish people from issues.* Build allegiances to people, not issues. Issues, like opinions, come and go. No point in getting too attached. But people are a different matter. People must always be the priority. That's why it's so important to keep

conflict in the Blue Zone. Red Zone conflict dissolves relationships, hurts people, and destroys organizations.

* *Distinguish symptoms from causes.* Another way to think about this is to center your feedback on observations, not on conclusions; on descriptions, not on judgments. When I jump to conclusions, invariably I'm also making judgments. And when I make judgments, I am ascribing intent. And when I ascribe intent, there's a good possibility I'm projecting out of my story. So instead of confronting you, I'm really confronting myself (in the person of you). And that gets confusing.

Conflict in a Group

We've talked about dealing with conflict between individuals. But what happens when conflict explodes within a group, a department, or a management team? Members of groups have a way of feeding each other's Red Zones. As a result, problem-solving turns into personal bashing, which is why people in organizations avoid conflicted issues. They fear that the conflict will turn personal and ugly. We've found a three-step process to be extremely helpful.

1. *Discourse.* During this phase, everyone is given a hearing. Each person takes a turn telling what he or she thinks about the situation. No one is allowed to comment on what is being said. We've found this stage to be critical, for usually when groups get into sustained conflict, people yell back and forth at one another, and no one is heard.

2. *Discussion.* During this phase, people are allowed to interact with each other. Each has heard fully the other participants' points of view. Now it is time to discuss these points. This is also a winnowing process in which the best ideas rise to the top and less useful concepts are discarded.

3. *Decision.* During this phase, a decision is made as to what direction the group needs to take or how the conflict is to be resolved. Specific action steps and timetables for implementation are generated.

When Heading into the Red Zone

We have found that most people who are successful in conflict not only manage to stay Blue Zone most of the time but also have learned to handle their Red Zone when it lurks in the shadows, ready to hijack the conflict. People who monitor their Red Zone tend to recover from distress more quickly than those who don't.

Consider Julio. He knows that he goes Red Zone with one particular manager—Franco—at his company. Julio knows that this fellow reminds him of a tormenting brother and that Julio's Red Zone issue is control. But still he tends to go Red Zone whenever Franco is around.

What Julio learned he needs to do whenever he finds himself going Red Zone with Franco is to excuse himself, go to the men's room, sit on a stool, and coach himself out of the mental place he is in.

Probably the most important strategy is to have the time to get a mental picture of what is occurring and to alter it. "I know I'm going Red Zone right now. My acceptance is not at stake."

The Most Important Questions to Ask to Stay Blue Zone

1. With whom do I tend to go Red Zone?
2. In what situations do I tend to go Red Zone?
3. What is my core Red Zone issue?
4. What strategy do I need to employ to get myself out of the Red Zone?

A question we are constantly asked is, What do I, as a leader, do when someone in a group setting is getting Red Zone? This is a common occurrence as a person begins to take the discussion personally.

Though each situation is different, there are several important principles to follow.

1. If a person is Red Zone but not disrupting the meeting, there is probably no reason to draw attention to the person. Drawing attention to the person may in fact ignite more Red Zone behavior.

2. Red Zone behavior tends to spread from one person to another. I go Red Zone, and I attack you. You go Red Zone and counterattack. Once two people have become locked in a Red Zone exchange, it's up to the leader to step in and halt the action. "You both are unable to focus effectively on the issue we're discussing. I suggest we take a break, and the two of you need to cool off and refocus."

Summary of Myths versus Truths

In parting, we'd like to share with you some myths and truths we've uncovered over the years in working with people. Most of these have been covered in the preceding pages, so you can treat this as a review.

MYTH	TRUTH
Others are much more "together" than I am.	Everyone is as fragile as I am.
New stories are constantly emerging.	There are no new stories, only variations.
My most important lessons are learned in successful relationships.	My most important lessons are learned in failed relationships.
Every statement people make is grounded outside of themselves.	Every statement people make is at least partially autobiographical.
I have only one story. I take it everywhere I go, and I can't change it, because the same things happen to me over and over.	I have a story that I was taught and now live, but it is up to me to examine it and make necessary changes.

continued on next page

continued from page 149

MYTH	TRUTH
Somebody else will give me the chance to change my story.	It's up to me to figure out my story and make necessary changes.
It's real easy to fix this mess.	Messes, especially relationship messes, are more complex than I think.
The way out is out.	The way out is inward.
The problem is out there, with them.	The problem is always in the room ... and begins with me.
The road to feeling better is a steadily upward movement toward pleasure.	The road to feeling better is through a certain amount of pain.
Life is easy.	Life is hard.
I'm at least as bad as I think I am, and everybody else knows it.	I'm better than I think I am and capable of more than I know.
My greatest resource is somewhere out there.	My greatest resource is myself.
If I want to know what's going on, I should look at the person.	If I want to know what's going on, I should look at the pattern.
I grow only when I am comfortable.	I grow only when I am uncomfortable.

Discussion Questions

Chapter 1

1. Given what you read about First Community, what would be some of the most challenging aspects of being its pastor?

2. What are some of the reasons that a one-time supporter might become a leader's nemesis?

3. Why did Elliott's words to Barry, "Are you sure you are cut out to be a pastor?" create so much rage in Barry? What do you think your response might be if someone asked you the same question about your job or career?

   Meditation: There are moments in all of our lives when we face a crisis that creates doubt in our ability to minister. What raises the doubts for you?

Chapter 2

1. What are the differences between technical change and adaptive change?

2. Do you think a church should be run like a business? Why or why not? Are there any aspects of business management that can be helpful in leading churches? If so, what are they?

3. Do you think a church should be led like a family? Why or why not?

4. In your own words, define a Red Zone leader. Then define a Blue Zone leader. Finally, define the difference between the two types of leaders.

   Meditation: As you reflect on your Red Zone behavior, what conflict is preventing you from realizing the success you've envisioned for your ministry?

Chapter 3

1. Do you agree with Elliott that Red Zone and Blue Zone issues are the same at home and at work? Why or why not?

2. Elliott argues that when we are in conflict with another, the real conflict lies within ourselves, not with the other person. Do you agree with this? Why or why not?

3. As Barry is leaving, Elliott says to him, "Every time I hear you talking about Jim Grendell, I hear you talking about yourself." What might Elliott mean?

   Meditation: Think about a Jim Grendell in your life, and the things you think and say about that person. Would Elliott say the same thing to you that he said to Barry?

Chapter 4

1. Where do you think Barry erred, if at all, as he introduced changes into his church?

2. How do you think Barry handled his meeting with Jim and the board? What do you think was driving Jim's concerns? What's your assessment of the way the other board members handled the meeting?

3. Who do you find yourself meeting, over and over again?

   Meditation: What within yourself is blocking you from examining the deeper issues that lie within?

Chapter 5

1. Barry states that the current evaluation of ministry success is attendance and membership, rate of church growth, and quality of church facilities. What is your evaluation of this comment? What standards do you use to measure your success in ministry?

2. How successful have you been in living up to your standards of success?

3. How often do you reevaluate the standards of success you use?

Meditation: What core issue within yourself has kept you from meeting your goals over the years? How does that issue relate to the "who" you meet over and over again (question 3 in chapter 4)?

Chapter 6

1. What links do you see between the difficulties Barry has at church and the difficulties he experiences with his son, Jake?

2. What do you think of the changes Barry proposed to the board? What's your reaction to the board's response to the changes?

3. What changes have you been considering at your church? What strategies have you considered to implement these changes? What is your hesitation in implementing them?

Meditation: In what ways do core issues within yourself block your ability to be fully present to your spouse, family, and friends?

Chapter 7

1. What is the difference between loving someone and approving of someone?

2. Why do you think that Barry, after the school principal shared his thoughts about Jake with him and Sophia, was sad and confused, and yet hopeful?

3. As he talked about transforming change, Elliott mentioned that Barry had the opportunity of a lifetime to provide for his son what Barry had never received from his own father. What was Elliott referring to?

Meditation: How many times, because of your fears, do you miss the opportunity to make a difference in the lives of those you love and serve?

Chapter 8

1. Because you are the pastor and leader of your church, do you feel primarily responsible for defining the vision and direction and for solving the challenges of your church?

2. Why are leaders of all organizations, not just churches, reluctant to challenge the values and beliefs of their congregation or community?

3. What do you think Elliott means when he speaks of the unspoken bargain that many pastors and congregations arrive at?

4. Do you think that vision is given to the pastor, or do you think vision is the shared vision of the community brought about in the crucible of conflict?

Meditation: What is the unrealized redemptive potential in the people you serve?

Chapter 9

1. As you consider challenging your congregation to live more fully in the Spirit, what do you think might be the "right questions," the hard questions to ask yourself and your congregation?

2. Are you willing to disappoint the expectations of those who look to you for answers and risk their disapproval?

3. Are you willing to maintain a relationship with someone who challenges you and your integrity so that you might help them with the challenges they face?

4. "When a person is at their most oppositional, that is the time when they are most vulnerable." What do you think that means for you and those who have entrusted themselves to you?

Meditation: Are you ready to face the fears within you and become a source of transformation and healing in your community? This is the challenge of becoming an adaptive-change pastor or leader: embrace the conflict within ourselves and accept our own flaws so that we can accept the flaws of others. This humility allow us to understand the conflicts that lie within others and to become a source of healing for them.

About TAG

AG (the Armstrong Group) is a management consulting firm in Fairfax, Virginia. Our organization is composed of a group of men and women who deeply believe that every person has the necessary internal resources to improve the quality of their lives by improving the quality of their relationships. What most people lack are the skills needed to utilize their gifts and talents. TAG's mission, to release the potential of every person and every organization and to allow them to discover possibilities, serves as the foundation for our approach to working with individuals, groups, and organizations. Our clients are large and small and from many different fields, including the federal government. Service is our lifelong focus. Our experience as mental-health therapists working directly with families, couples, individuals, and especially pastors has prepared us for the work we do today.

TAG partners and associates coach pastors from around the country and in Canada. TAG also conducts a TAG Leadership Institute for active pastors. The leadership institute is an intense two-day program designed to allow pastors to work with the concepts presented in this book. If you would like to sponsor a leadership institute or participate in one, or would like more information about the work we do with pastors, their congregations, and their churches, please contact us:

Phone: 1-877-TAGLINE
Website: www.877tagline.com
James Osterhaus: josterhaus@877tagline.com
Joseph Jurkowski: jjurkowski@877tagline.com
Todd Hahn: todd@psieducation.com

Jim Osterhaus, PhD (Partner, Consultant). Jim Osterhaus is a senior partner with TAG. He is a dynamic executive coach and public speaker with extensive experience in helping individuals move through change, conflict, and reorganization. He brings a depth of understanding of systems and relational-network thinking to his work, developed from years of practicing as a highly respected psychologist in northern Virginia, in addition to consulting. His experience includes serving on a special commission established by the vice president of the United States to consider the emotional effects of government downsizing, facilitation of the Organizational Culture component of the Army Staff Redesign, and workshop development and implementation for clients from the East Coast to the West Coast. He was recently interviewed by Sam Donaldson (ABC News) as a leading expert in organizational issues. He has been quoted in the *New York Times*, *Los Angeles Times*, *Seattle Times*, and many other leading publications.

He has facilitated groups and taught seminars in numerous settings, including the University of San Francisco, American University, Denver Seminary, Bethel Seminary, and Trinity Episcopal School for Ministry. Jim has authored seven books and written dozens of articles for magazines and trade journals. His latest book, coauthored with Kevin Ford, is *The Thing in the Bushes: Turning Organizational Blind Spots into Competitive Advantage* (Pinon Press). The book was listed among Amazon.com's top 900 in sales in June 2002 and was featured by Bill Hybels in Willow Creek's leadership conference as one of the ten best leadership books of that year.

Jim is a well-respected leader in many circles. He has demonstrated achievement as an entrepreneur and has the unique ability to bring a group of people to a deep sense of personal ownership. He holds a PhD in counseling psychology from American University and degrees in counseling from Virginia Polytechnic Institute and Catholic University.

Joe Jurkowski (Managing Partner, President). Joe is the president and chief mobilization officer for TAG. He is a strategic thinker, a leader in applying systems theory in organizational settings, an entrepreneur, and a well-respected leader in his work with the federal government. His expertise in understanding systems theory is unparalleled. He has provided extensive executive coaching and conflict management with the Federal Aviation Administration, the U.S. Army (Office of the Chief of Staff), Kaiser Permanente, U.S. Customs, and many other large and small organizations. He is a master consultant who can reframe complex organizational problems in ways that mobilize leadership. He has consulted with family-owned businesses, financial institutions, managed-care organizations, and physician practices.

As a recognized national leader in resolving organizational conflict, Joe has worked confidentially with Fortune 500 executives across the nation.

He has provided executive-coaching and conflict-resolution services to some of the nation's most prominent business and political leaders. Joe has been quoted extensively in the press as an expert on organizational development. He has appeared in diverse publications, including *Entrepreneur*, the *Cincinnati Enquirer*, the *Washington Post*, and *CU Times*.

Joe earned his master's degree in psychological counseling from the University of Maryland in 1970 and began working as a therapist in a residential treatment center for adolescents. He became director of the program in 1973 and designed a treatment approach that created incentives for positive behavior. In 1978 he was appointed director of family therapy at Karma Academy, a residential treatment center for adolescents with substance abuse problems. In 1978 he entered the extern program at the Philadelphia Child guidance clinic, where he studied structural family therapy with Salvador Minuchin and Jay Haley. After postgraduate work at the child guidance clinic, Joe became the director of the Children and Family Services Partial Hospitalization unit at the Mt. Vernon Community Mental Health Center. While at Mt. Vernon, he taught the family therapy seminar and served as the liaison with Child Protective Services for all child abuse cases in the Mt. Vernon catchment area. In 1983 Joe entered private practice and began working primarily with families and couples. In 1991 he founded the Counseling Center of Fairfax in an effort to develop a community of therapists who could support each other's growth and development and serve the community of Fairfax with a shared set of values. Joe is one of the founding partners of TAG.

Todd Hahn (Partner, Consultant). Todd is the president of couchhead.com and PSI Resources. Deeply experienced in hands-on leadership in the not-for-profit sector as well as in parish ministry, Todd is one of the nation's leading thinkers on the shift from the modern era to the postmodern era and its implications for organizations and organizational leadership. Skilled as a facilitator and at bringing clarity, momentum, and focus to organizational planning, Todd has consulted with a wide variety of organizations on how leadership works in the postmodern era and how business leaders can help their organizations navigate the rapidly changing cultural landscape.

Todd's strengths as a consultant include helping an organization sharpen and hone its focus and direction; troubleshooting the factors that slow an organization's growth; building energy, enthusiasm, and unity among executive teams; and assisting organizations to crystallize their vision along with action steps to get them there.

Todd has worked with government clients, including the Federal Aviation Administration and Arlington County (Virginia). His specialty is working with churches. He is nationally recognized as an expert on helping churches understand and reach Generation X, adding and programming alternative worship services, and coaching churches through church planting and satellite campus development. He is widely known for his speaking at workshops and conferences at the denominational level and in the local-church context, as well as for planting one of the nation's fastest growing and innovative churches, in North Carolina.

Todd is the coauthor of two books on the values, aspirations, and spirituality of Generation X and is the author of a book on followership in both the for-profit and not-for-profit sectors. He has been widely quoted in the media, including the *Miami Herald*, the *Charlotte Observer*, the *Los Angeles Times*, the *New Orleans Times-Picayune*, *Christianity Today*, and *Leadership*. He is currently writing a book on adoption.

Todd has a BA from the University of North Carolina at Chapel Hill, and a master of divinity from Gordon-Conwell Theological Seminary.